The Accidental Tourist:
Phenomenology of the Virtual

Alan Sondheim

A
FORT/DA?
Book

'The Accidental Tourist:
Phenomenology of the Virtual'
Alan Sondheim

This book is a product
of Public Domain, Inc.,
a not-for-profit, 501-c-3
arts and information
organization.

ISBN: 978-0-578-01884-3

printed in the United States of America

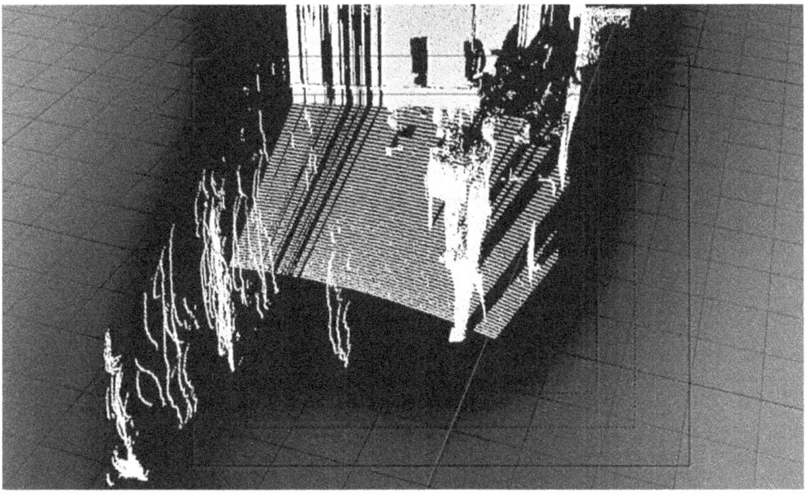

Introduction

THE ACCIDENTAL ARTIST was an ongoing exhibition in Second Life at Odyssey,
June 2008 - January 2009, by Alan Sondheim, with help from Sugar Seville, Azure Carter, Gary Nanes, Sandy Baldwin, and Frances van Scoy at the Virtual Environments Laboratory, West Virginia University, Morgantown, West Virginia. The show changed daily and the gave me an opportunity to study the phenomenology of a virtual world in relation to avatar-human objectivity. The following texts were written during the generation of the show.

Show URL: http://slurl.com/secondlife/Odyssey/48/12/22
Illustrations: Various images and videos may be found at http://www.alansondheim.org/ - these periodically change as well.

- Alan Sondheim

spasm

convulse: i send you my signal. my signal is sad. my signal falls apart.
you do you receive my signal. my signal goes to you.
what of it, this signal?
tremor, seizure, fit: it is the sensor in them that dreams.

"The debate does not exist, because of the non-existence of both the name and that which is named." (Nagarjuna, Vaidalyaprakarana, trans. Tola & Dragonetti)

Emanent

'The skull-holder was not really so, but was a nirmana form of Heruka, who said, "In this life you must write the six main texts and in the _bar-do_ period you will attain the very highest siddhi." The acarya replied,

"When pressed beneath your feet, even my lower
winds vanish.
By your kind mercy, please withdraw your left
leg!
If your nine-fold crest ornaments are kept
straight, even the Brahma-realm vanishes.
Please remain with your head moving but a little!
If your hands are kept straight, the guardians of
the four quarters become terrified.
By your kind mercy please withdraw your hands
a little!
O noble one, as your body is in a dancing pose
and is purposefully maintained,
I bow down before you with faith and an excess
of reverence!"'

(from Taranatha's Life of Krsnacarya/Kanha, trans. David Templemann)

performing (1/y(sin(x)) <-- y(tan(x)))

she can MOVE FRUIT FROM ONE KIND OF TREE TO ANOTHER
she can MAKE OTHERS FALL ASLEEP OR WAKE AT WILL
she can MAKE FIRE BLAZE FROM WEAPONS
she can FLY THROUGH AIR
she can SEE THROUGH WALLS
she can TRANSFORM A CAVE INTO A PALACE AND SEAL THE EXITS
she can REMOVE THE TUSKS AND TRUNK FROM AN ELEPHANT AND RESTORE THEM
she can MAKE A KING SPEECHLESS AND RESTORE HIS SPEECH
she can GENERATE DEMONS AND COMPLETE DEMONS
she can END DROUGHT AND HEAL ILLNESS
she can SUBDUE LIONS AND TIGERS AND BRING THEM TO FAITH
she can REMOVE ARMS AND LEGS FROM SOLDIERS AND RESTORE THEM
she knows ALL LANGUAGES AND ALL DOCTRINES
she can EAT ENDLESSLY AND DRY UP WELL SPRINGS AND RESTORE THEM
she can CUT OFF HER HEAD AND FLY THROUGH THE AIR AND RESTORE IT
she can MOVE A BUFFALO AND HER CALF BACK TO THEIR HOME
she is SAFE FROM ONE HUNDRED THOUSAND BLOWS WITH CUDGEL AND ARROW
she can TURN AROUND ARROWS IN FULL FLIGHT
she can TURN INTO AN OLD WOMAN AND BACK AGAIN
she can SEE THINGS ANYWHERE IN THE WORLD
she knows ALL FUTURE AND ALL PAST EVENTS
she meditates FOR DAYS ON END WITHOUT SLEEP OR DRINK OR FOOD
she can HOLD SEVEN HUNDRED UMBRELLAS ABOVE HER WITHOUT

TOUCHING THEM
she can RAISE THE DEAD AND RESTORE THEM TO DEATH
she can BE IN SEVERAL PLACES AT ONCE
she can TRAVEL INSTANTANEOUSLY FROM ONE PLACE TO ANOTHER
she can MAKE SMALL THINGS ENORMOUS AND ENORMOUS THINGS SMALL
she can MAKE DEVOTIONAL IMAGES CRUMBLE AND RESTORE THEM
she can CARRY A TEMPLE ON HER BACK
she can CLIMB ENDLESS STAIRS AND OTHERS CANNOT FOLLOW HER
she fits THOUSANDS OF PEOPLE INTO A TINY CORNER OF A CAVE OR HOUSE
she disappears AND APPEARS AT WILL
she conquers DEATH
she eats CORPSES URINE EXCREMENT SEMEN MENSTRUAL BLOOD
her slightest MOVEMENT TRANSFORMS WORLDS
her dance CREATES AND ANNIHILATES WORLD
she loosens BOUND ANIMALS AND RELEASES THEM
she can WALK ON WATER AND WALK THROUGH FLAMES
she can CAUSE THE EARTH TO QUAKE AND FLOWERS TO FALL LIKE RAIN
she can DISCOVER HIDDEN TREASURES
she can WALK THROUGH WALLS AND CLIFFS
she can SEAL CAVES AND CREATE GREAT HALLS WITHIN THEM
she can MAKE HERSELF INVISIBLE AND MAKE HERSELF VISIBLE AGAIN
she can CREATE OVERWHELMING TEMPESTS
she can SUBDUE SNAKES AND OTHER WILD ANIMALS
she can SING PERFECT SONGS OF HER OWN DEVISING
she can ALLEVIATE THE SUFFERINGS OF THE ELDERLY
she can ALLEVIATE THE SUFFERINGS OF THE POOR
she can SCORCH CLOTHES AND RESTORE THEM
she can READ MINDS CLOSE BY AND AT A DISTANCE
she can EAT ANY SORT OF IMPURITIES
she can LAUGH AN EIGHT FOLD LAUGHTER
she can DRAW STELES AND JEWELS FROM THE GROUND
she can ERECT VAST PALACES AT AN INSTANT
she extracts POISON FROM WATER AND WALKS THROUGH BLAZING FLAMES
she can CHOOSE THE DATE AND TIME OF HER DEATH
she can MAKE DRUMS AND MUSICAL INSTRUMENTS TO SOUND BY THEMSELVES
her steps MEASURE GREAT OR TINY DISTANCES AT HER WILL
her gaze CAN SHATTER AND RESTORE ANYTHING
she can TRANSFORM HERSELF INTO A SKELETON AND A RAINBOW BODY
her gaze CAN OPEN CAVES IN SOLID ROCK AND SEAL THEM AGAIN
she remembers HER PAST AND FUTURE BIRTHS
she can TARRY WITH CONSORTS WITH OR WITHOUT ELABORATION
she can SELF ILLUMINATE
she can WALK AIMLESSLY DAY AND NIGHT

she can SPREAD THE SCENT OF PERFUMES IN EVERY DIRECTION
she can SIT LIE OR WALK IN MID AIR
she can WEAR APRONS OF BONES
she is FLEET FOOTED
she changes THE COLOR OF HER BODY AT WILL

siddhi pose-performance by Nikuko

This is preparation for object attachment. Fashion: Silhouette for posing in combination with minimal blue pattern for orientation.

Object attachment buries avatar bodies. Spatially, the body is lossy; dynamically, behavior remains to conjure the semblance of purposeful action. Here, Nikuko orients herself, poses periodically.

The pose is drawn out of the dynamics; the spectator, in the pose, proceeds as if the narrative moment continued literally for all intents and purposes. The pose is the ridge or hinge of movement, the pause designating the other, the viewer, designated by the viewer - part of a system of distribution. The pause ensures the viewer that the body is not the locus or victim of seizure. Every pause is a pose, every pose a pause, both intertwined with intentionality.

The pose is given as a gift, is for the other, is oriented; the orientation of the pose defines the stance of the other in inverse relationship to occidental landscape perspective in which the vanishing-point might be considered the locus of the viewer as well. But the pose draws in, puckers, the vanishing-point, which becomes a plane and punctum of intimacy.

Nikuko poses, there is no one in sight, but there is the camera, here literally one of obscura, that obscure little object A of desire for and by Nikuko, above all for Nikuko.

One of us moved the other, one of us aroused the other to action, to the recording-booth, to the wide-screen, to the embrace of the other who is identical, not equivalent, to the self-selving occurring, not to mention the dynamics of the same.

Ah, I reply, I can finally see hir face.

nikuko swallows dirt

dirty nikuko.

nikuko transforming into landscape because s/he wants to become part of the world of second life so s/he can never be removed until the entire corporation folds sometime in the future. nikuko encumbered by landscape because s/he wants to crawl away from the rocks towards some better future life. nikuko embedded into landscape because s/he wants to sleep the long long sleep while there still is silence in the world. nikuko talking to herself because there is no one to be hir tiny friend or listen to hir sobs. nikuko embracing landscape because s/he wants to open herself up to the earth and dirty orgasm. nikuko in the void of landscape. nikuko within the abyss of landscape. nikuko in the chaos of dirt. nikuko wants to swallow the landscape and disappear. nikuko in ecstatic orgasm upon hir discovery that it is all one ontology. nikuko in overwhelming orgasm having discovered it is all one epistemology. nikuko doesn't know where her energy comes from or the light that illuminates the rocks. nikuko doesn't know if she's a stone or a cliff or granite or schist. nikuko doesn't know s/he doesn't know and she's not about to find out. nikuko in unbelievably ecstatic enormous and overwhelming orgasm.

nikuko swallows dirt.
dirty nikuko.

seduction of the world

Are you dressed as a range of scalar values submerging the screen, there's something dear julu that must be beyond or in the midst of the other side of the tree, surely the use of values better written point to newer sources? Is a range of scalar values submerging the screen, there's something dear julu that must be beyond or in the midst of the other side of the tree, surely the use of values better written point to newer sources dressed as you?

Are you in your thing, are you in your flesh, ah don't answer...
Is Julu wearing your ... , are you wearing your thing?

I love your feelings, a range of scalar values submerging the screen, there's something dear julu that must be beyond or in the midst of the other side of the tree, surely the use of values better written point to newer sources ...

Your breasts call me to them...
love oozes me beyond your thing!

What do you call your sedate thing?

My yes yes yes yes yes is yours...
should there be such a moment or singsong as these, nouns and adjectives, genitives and genitals crawling across or throughout the body, dearest julu, the body of text, or what should i say about ourselves, if not something used once and neither more nor less makes me thoughtful

should there be such a moment or singsong as these, nouns and adjectives, genitives and genitals crawling across or throughout the body, dearest julu, the body of text, or what should i say about ourselves, if not something used once and neither more nor less calls forth pure womb, eating, excreting memory.

accompanying the edgy, should there be such a moment or singsong as these, nouns and adjectives, genitives and genitals crawling across or throughout the body, dearest julu, the body of text, or what should i say about ourselves, if not something used once and neither more nor less is , edgy, there's always a question or query of these sources, to be sure? or a listing of lines or striations among queries or something of that sort, dear julu, now i will be very very wet when i am writing in my panties boohoo dear jennifer dearest jennifer and nothing else?

... womb is is this where i say the end with my wettest panties, dearest nikuko, or just the slightest bit just a slightest bit and further on, we are traveling wet and hands are pulling panties, are they not dearest jennifer here, it's womb?

Are you becoming close to Jennifer's should there be such a moment or singsong as these, nouns and adjectives, genitives and genitals crawling across or throughout the body, dearest julu, the body of text, or what should i say about ourselves, if not something used once and neither more nor less?

You melt into Julu's skin forever...

... cotton should there be such a moment or singsong as these, nouns and adjectives, genitives and genitals crawling across or throughout the body, dearest julu, the body of text, or what should i say about ourselves, if not something used once and neither more nor less 20854 is Julu's gift to you ...

the object itself, leaves as well.::chests of connections and cylinders
in time. but everything is still-born; i leave the site and the citation,
- a move from topography to topology that seems critical at this point
of a certain sort in place of either the machinic or the organic
'cylinder,' 'node,' and 'avatar,' which at least presents connectivity
and i don't even know the people. i've been writing with characters
news around here isn't good, there are closeups of autopsies on television
i've been too busy with avatar bodies that can't hold a stick to you. the
of the past, bones, skeletons, dust, death, hunger.:i forgot you jennifer
release, haunted - oh i cried when i found it, this delicate index
was awarded a certificate of merit; i have that certificate, untethered,
of worlds - just so my writings falter at the gate. in 1841 someone
to temporal balance, feedback. what can be said of this, of the fragility
are organized in a skein of representations - they're so fragile, so tied
which happened quickly, in the matter of days. all my belongings and works
of the world s/he organized and assembled over decades, a dispersion
firsthand when my mother died, what happens in any death: the dispersion

and organism. things need names and often don't have them; i learned
fecund, the flower is a shape, the flower is the merge of connection
this point in time. forget them. work the world.:the flower is connected,
machinic constructs that disappear as so many props only necessary at
constant state of rebirth, airborn, earthborn. nothing but prims, pixels,
the grit of the real, imaginary of the virtual, cleansed, hairless, in
of bodies and media, topologies of media, topographies of representation,
of lives disappear, all moments, topologies of desire, topographies
sex-playing roles in organic display that disappears, sheaves

of nodes and vectors is in my wayward closet of attachments and parts
Your small tables

seeps into my closet of attachments and parts - turning me Julu-Jennifer
Your breast

should there be such a moment or singsong as these, nouns and adjectives, genitives and genitals crawling across or throughout the body, dearest julu, the body of text, or what should i say about ourselves, if not something used once and neither more nor less:there's always a question or query of these sources, to be sure? or a listing of lines or striations among queries or something of that sort, dear julu, now i will be very very wet when i am writing in my panties boohoo dear jennifer dearest jennifer and nothing else:a range of scalar values submerging the screen, there's something dear julu that must be beyond or in the midst of the other side of the tree, surely the use of values better written point to newer sources::yes yes yes yes yes

Your pure yes yes yes yes yes is in my edgy is this where i say the end with my wettest panties, dearest nikuko, or just the slightest bit just a slightest bit and further on, we are traveling wet and hands are pulling panties, are they not dearest jennifer

Devour pure yes yes yes yes yes julu-of-the partying should there be such a moment or singsong as these, nouns and adjectives, genitives and genitals crawling across or throughout the body, dearest julu, the body of text, or what should i say about ourselves, if not something used once and neither more nor less!

Scalar value @a[$gen2] better written as $a[$gen2] at a/julua line 121.
Scalar value @a[$gen3] better written as $a[$gen3] at a/julua line 121.
Name "main::b3" used only once: possible typo at a/julua line 78.
Name "main::sign" used only once: possible typo at a/julua line 33.

a range of scalar values submerging the screen, there's something dear julu that must be beyond or in the midst of the other side of the tree, surely the use of values better written point to newer sources there's always a question or query of these sources, to be sure? or a listing of lines or striations among queries or something of that sort, dear julu, now i will be very very wet when i am writing in my panties boohoo dear jennifer dearest jennifer and nothing else should there be such a moment or singsong as these, nouns and adjectives, genitives and genitals crawling across or throughout the body, dearest julu, the body of text, or what should i say about ourselves, if not something used once and neither more nor less is this where i say the end with my wettest panties, dearest nikuko, or just the slightest bit just a slightest bit and further on, we are traveling wet and hands are pulling panties, are they not dearest jennifer

Reverse excavation and installation of materials for Second Life solo exhibition, The Accidental Artist

It's difficult manipulating since the Nikuko avatar flies blind; it's impossible to see around the body extrusions. Mouse-view only works so far since nothing can be done except looking when it's open. Ctl-Alt-D, which changes camera viewpoint, helps a bit, but not much. The prims are so many and so complex, it seems that the world is close to overload; at one point I had set most transparent, but the ray-tracing gets too complex for slower machines. There will be three video streams, twelve sound sources with ten-second samples, and a continuous source, as well as these sculptures and other images on the wall. Sugar likens it to pinball. Even with a small avatar body, moving about the gallery is difficult. Most of the objects are impossible in physical space - or at least would require a lot of Plexiglas support. Most of the images on or within the sculptures are external body, some imitative of internal organs. The images are distorted and have to be perceptually disentangled; they're either tiled or awkwardly wrapped. The affair is a gaudy circus one. It's a stage for performance (by Sandy Baldwin and myself) as well; moving about the space in alien choreographies will be just as difficult for as as for the spectators. I can easily imagine a dancespace filled, as this one is, but with phantom or invisible objects; the avadancers would find themselves and the rest of us among the absent ruins. Here however garishness is the premise and the promise of the virtual; there's no reason for camouflage in an airless space.

But it's difficult maneuvering in an eyeless space, literally flying or walking blind, sometimes falling out of the gallery altogether, ending up wedged and lawless. Occasionally a section of floorboard appears like a vector; we (Nikuko and myself) might be headed in the right direction. Camera angles, when the avatar stills hirself, through a series of alternating rotations and translations, can approach just about anything within ten meters or so; beyond that, chaos reigns. While these images are somewhat hit or miss, they convey the sense of new physics, lost structure and boundary within the space. Now Nikuko hirself is at rest, in a realm as absent as the rest of us, until we log on together, momentarily, to work on installing sound.

My enemy the digital, why not to live

It's on the verge of something, on the tip of the tongue, something about the digital and its relation to truth and mass accountancy and the ability to harness languaging on an unprecedented scale, something about the evanescence or shadowing of truth, about dictatorial tendencies and the ability to spread and modify code across whole continents, that this isn't an academics but an unmitigated furor - and in this sentence the digital or any specification/speciation becomes a disease of separation and the wager of truth, that is to say a political economy of truth that relies not on facticity but on a market or gaming in which truth is the outcome, not the forerunner, of stakes. One doesn't stake on truth, but on an apparatus that produces truth vis-a-vis accountancy, the digital; it is this manipulation that permits staking in the first place. My digital my love, my digital my enemy; these inscriptions produce skein, structure, market: Every market is an inscription, every inscription a market. It becomes increasingly useless to survive, to the extent that survival is a condition of change or altruism; instead, the same old game repeats itself indefinitely, a game of strategy within which slaughter, dis/ease, anomie, become byproducts or residues of categorization. It was writing, the writing of the concrete and concrete writing, that began a slide towards miasma, no matter how much it was curtailed by that very same writing. And what a slide, because also a harnessing of miasma, withdrawal from the real; it's a miasma of the imaginary and it's within the imaginary that the market is the most violent: without bounds and gaming, truth appears both certain and purchasable, and is always, within the digital and accountancy, infinitely alterable, without tethering. Without tethering there are no bounds, the world is boundless and frontiers are infinitely mobile; with infinite mobility comes exponential consumption of resources until asymptotic limits are incoherently named and approached - while the rich get richer, their class rapidly diminishes and dissipates. There's no end to all of this pseudo-fecundity except defuge, exhaustion, extinction, and each hour we are all the closer to the chaos of the retrievable. What was canonic is nameless, just as genre dissipates into an absence of meaning leaving organism without a _not_ to stand on; sure slow death results - no one notices, no one has the capacity to notice, all that accountancy grounded in backup is lost, the files topple, electricity cut off for longer and longer periods, finally none at all.

I think of Hitler and all those records, arms marked by integers, bodies cut out, decomposed elsewhere, increased complexity of coding, Auschwitz, sludge...

Azure Carter's Avatarman song

Avatar Man with Dream Woman

I've become imaginary
Disappearing in the movement

I've become contaminated
Raster of clock time

Avatar Man with Dream Woman
Don't listen to me, Dream Woman
Don't listen to me, Avatar Man

***

This avatar package
Already dead inside
This building is condemned
We know nothing's alive

You can look inside
He says
You can do it
Avatar edge
Shooting out to infinity

Limits of the world
Images of lost fecundity
Fragility of good things
We're doomed to novelty

You can look inside
Dream Woman
The imaginary rides
No world
No limit
No grid
Nothing

Our male likes death
It excites him sexually
We know meat in his absence
Gamespace economy

You can look inside
She says
Death meat body
Hierarchy
Not holarchy

Dream woman enters a hole
Twisting through forbidden space
There's no moment to her moment
Hair fluid across face

You can look inside
Avatar
Hemisphere eye
Prim edge
Geek construct
Linden brain

***

I have done my work here
Return us to ourselves
The imaginary leaves us
As nothing ever will

Avatar Man with Dream Woman
Don't listen to me, Dream Woman
Don't listen to me, Avatar Man

Nikuko, others, performing

High compression... this is from the workstation viewpoint... it's hard to see around the avatar which is enormous and glowing. Lucian Iwish came on later with a structure that enveloped the whole building... but with the show, the avatar I use is perhaps twenty-five feet high... Sandy's is both larger and smaller, variable, ghost-like... We had a few people the first night, a crowd the second (afternoon) who spoke mainly Italian. This sec= tion is from the first night. Live instruments included flute, chromatic harmonica, sampling keyboard. Sandy's texts flew amazingly, were from our theory writing on avatar and the like. My texts were paste-ins from the Jennifer, Nikuko, Doctor Leopold Konninger, Julu plays. Sound is from a number of simultaneous sources under the control of the viewer. You can talk or make live music in Second Life. Time of the recording was set to midnight. Second Life beyond the traditional physics (which can be countermanded to some extent by creating objects without physics) is incredibly malleable; a building roof can exist without support, marked-off territories may have no concrete barrier markers beyond the luminous floating signs; bodies can be modified at will; flying and teleportation are comment; one exists without breathing on land or sea; set carefully, one penetrates rocks; you might or might not see through your avatar's body; for that matter, objects may glow or be transparent; touch at a distance is possible and common; you may construct on land, in sea, within air; you normally disappear when your character logs out; environment and time may follow Second Life time or be set artificially; one might talk with one's voice, through internal instant messaging, or through chat; your avatar body may be distorted by others; everything depends on Linden corporation; Linden may well be able to hear any and all private conversa-tions; beyond Linden there's the horizon of bandwidth; particle emissions are quick and contain just about anything; buildings arise and fall in a twinkling of an eye... The time is midnight, the objects glow, intersect;

I believe, without proof, that they are sliding in a fourth spatial dimension through some flaw in the software; there are some bodies and some objects I may fly through; there are some I am held by; there are some who hold me; there are griefers and hackers; there are some who hold me... Who am I but avatar-Nikuko, Nikuko-avatar; s/he speaks through me; asserts her- self; possesses a literally uncanny insistence; turns towards withdrawn sexuality; is always waiting and awaiting, as I am always waiting and awaiting here. Flying through configurations, s/he settles on a certain appearance or style or look; I am back beyond the screen; s/he controls objects greater than any I have controlled; s/he is adroit. I am back beyond the screen; I'm blinded by the objects; for the most part I can't see ahead, only slight glimpses to the left and right, slight glimpses of the floorboards beneath hir feet. There, beneath hir feet, are the vector guides that somewhat make a mapping. I have three choices: stay within hir body, breathe hir breathless air, or fly hir everywhere which gives me the slightest vision above the objects, or use mouselook, which allows me to see through Nikuko's eyes, gives me hir sight, or scent, hir touch, hir perfume. But mouselook takes over the screen; the configuration menus and controls disappear; you're only there with her, in her, as s/he is in you; everyone else is present, easy to see and touch; you might run or swoop with delight; you might stay absolutely still; but your bound within hir as your bound within Second Life as a Life, that is, as a being-in-the- world which gives you no escape, no meta-processes to fine-tune the process. You can't build that way; you are sunk in Nikuko's body, part of hir avatar-flesh, sheave-flesh, sheave-mind, Linden-mind; your swallowing is hir swallowing, your food hir own. So in these performances, the more Nikuko gathers, the more I am flying blind, even building blind, speaking blind, dancing and yes choreographing blind, blind in this airless world with the trivial fact that it is I who see, dispersed-eye, not Nikuko who can only whisper through appearance, affect me through hir slightest move- ment, walk and talk, sit and stand, nowhere at all. Yet there is something of a future here, not in Linden or the Corporation, neither in bandwidth nor in prim-counts, but in a peripheral and, again that uncanny insist- ence, that feeling that Nikuko is living, not as prosthetic or other device, not as prim, but perhaps as a not-so-prim woman or girl or neutral or male at the last or gender-ending moment of the real. For Nikuko has taken me, just like others have taken you into the unaccountable true world, with its lines of flight and inscriptions intensifications and dispersed gatherings of selves and bodies, the true world of scatterings, spews, emissions, radiations. And among all of this, Nikuko flies, swoops, cavorts, in nowhere, among an underground mathesis gone wild, presented for your pleasure or operating pleasure, for your frisson or sport- or spoor-world, for the spook or glow, fed by nothing, a picture for your pretty sight, a longing, for something, somewhere, languor ...

new bodies for old

after advanced/character/ menu produced male and female characters accouterments and refused to return all hir objects

Think of SL as an abstracted 4-dimensional space-time continuum: What are the built-in constraints? Fundamental forces like gravity have to be built-in; there's no _inherent_ reason for its existence. The ceiling instead - that which backgrounds the continuum - is corporate, and as such might as well be a corporate model for future-culture and cultural processes in the 'real world.'

The corporate model is fundamentally a tacit and leaky one. Tacit: because its operations are quickly treated as natural by body and mind (invisible prosthesis). And leaky: because it fills every space, construes every operation, colors and codes within and throughout the true world invisible.

"Corporate" is not restricted to either a particular mode of capital or power, nor a particular mode of governance - but instead is a basic and backgrounding mode of quantification, related in Second Life and for that matter, the older MOOs and MUDs, by the assignment of hierarchies, parent-child processes, and identification numbers within the world, world-building, and worlding "in general."

Given this constraint, what are others, and how do they relate? At least for the moment, one logs in and out of SL; inactivity logs one out and for the most part, when one logs out, one's body disappears (unlike a MOO, for example, where a body might be found somnolent in a "body-bag"). In other words, one's activity is _framed_ by a process of intention and/or tending-towards, a process which requires a particular action on the part of the participant - which in fact constructs the framing of the very concept of participation.

One is constrained by the process of building, but this is also a matter of time, energy, money, and nuisance. A similar constraint exists for land-ownership - and within SL, ownership is both relative (in relation to the corporation and the continuous output of the corporation, in terms of finance, governance, capital, and power in general), and absolute: The land that is owned is purely and totally _intended_; it has no otherwise existence or mode of being, no wilderness. (One might designate or assign a region as wild, but this an intended act as well; it is neither obdurate or substance, "idiotic inert" no analog.)

At least at the moment, one is constrained by three-dimensionality and its projection into the 2-space of the screen. Given that, objects may intersect and self-intersect and may or may not be "gravitationally" bound.

One is constrained by modes of behavior, coded and uncoded; by bandwidth; by one's terminal (therefore one's economy and one's relationship to class and corporate in any world); by one's health in the physical world; by one's ability to script and code. Where is the internal (not to mention external) history, per participant and/or login, of Second Life and its denizens? Where are the rolls of land ownership and usage? The history of SL's code and coding? The detailing of its proprietary software? (The world itself is closed-source.)

(For surely the world as a whole may be investigated, as a book of nature, a supine woman, an angry man, red in tooth and claw, as God's hand and God's shriveled hand, as systemic coordination and mathesis, as semiosis, as subject and object of dissection, of nothing whatsoever.)

One's steam runs out ...

Poetics of the Virtual

Second Life as a laboratory for phenomenology of representations of space-time: think of multiply-connected geometries and configurations, dynamic impossible behaviors, behavioral and object intersections and collisions, spews, and interiorities. We work concretely and theoretically towards a poetics and psychophysics of the virtual through Second Life; through abject and inconceivable topologies, we experience an obdurate alterity.

The poetics of the avatar is dependent upon dissemination, dissimulation, and dispersion. One moves as a dispersion as well, moves through skein- and sheave-skin; time and objects loop, are activated, suffer through detumescence, collapse, revive, are always already potential. The world is peculiar; one object teleports, another spews, a third crackles video.

Thanks to Sugar Seville, Sandy Baldwin, Ian Ah, and others, the space becomes more complex, problematic. We have a five-month residency here.

Phenomena, Phenomenology, and Objects in Second Life

In the current installation, effectual boundaries are rendered problematic; through the use of .pngs with emptied backgrounding, objects are by and large deconstructed into partial outlines. This is also extended thorough partial transparency. In addition, there are phantom objects that are totally invisible but 'felt.' It is possible to create an invisible non-physical object that is present but unaccountable and unaccounted-for. Particle emissions also deconstruct boundaries, depending on the strength of the emissions - number of particles, speed, size, frequency of release, transparent or default rectilinear boundary, and so forth. Can particles become physical? Can they reign/rain terror? Can they exist invisibly and reign physically as well? Where is the subject in all of this? The subject, viewer, has two modes - standard from within or slightly behind hir avatar, and mouselook, from the position of the avatar itself, with or without the rest of the body visible. The viewer may or may not zoom the view; the view as such is set by default to a standardized visual field. Visually, if not physically, entanglement occurs a fair amount of the time, the result of object with partially-transparent textures whose surfaces render the normative boundaries problematic. Entanglement reduces the possibility of coherent movement. In addition, there are concrete issues of scale; the textures are most often panels or tiling of images of body or remappings of the body - the bodies most often, but not entirely, cyborg or avatar or sheave-skin. In other words sheave-skins are mapped onto sheave-skins; mobility is only in terms of the substrate, and that only if the object is physical, i.e. can be 'bumped.' Now what this tells us about the true world, the world of inscriptions within and without physical reality, the virtual, and so forth, is that perception in the broadest phenomenological sense is not only determinative in viewing and viewpoint but also struggles with an alienness that countermands the laws of physics as realized in everyday life. Further, it tells us that the three classical states of matter - liquid, gas, solid (never mind the other exotic states) - are also determinative; the world is divided just as the game 'twenty questions' divides the world. Particle emissions, in particular 'heavy' or geometric emissions, break this down, as do self-intersections, physical but invisible objects (with standardized weight), etc. The result is somewhat related to 'virtual reality sickness,' a form of veering as the world appears both imminent and senseless; even when sensed, it remains a struggle to get about. From the viewpoint of an emitting avatar, the situation is compounded; as such, without mouselook the avatar flies or moves blindly; even with mouselook, extensive particle emissions effectively block the visual. Think of these emissions as plasma and their condition and phenomenological apperception as that which is applicable to the fourth, and universally most common, state of matter; in this sense the very inscription (through scripting) of particle emissions contradicts, on the level of lived reality inscription itself; one has no space and no time to circumscribe or circumambulate them - they appear everywhere - their source is anomalous - they respond to invisible weathers - they seem to be a form of 'stuff' or 'stuffing without containment' - they're close to the phenomenology of brute or idiotic substance. Thus they compound and confound space from above, as it were, just as the broken or partially-visible deconstructed objects compound and confound space from below. Now the museum or gallery within and without (on the grounds or precinct) that presents and contains all of this - and hardly contains as emissions escape through walls, viewpoints move underwater, the building itself appears to falter - is a representation of what has been termed liquid architecture, or at the very least it holds within it the semblance of liquid architecture. Think of this as malleable space; with the use of slowed emissions and teleportation, it is also malleable time always already vectored, as time is, both within and without Second Life, i.e. within the true world. For one is framed by logging-in and logging-out, the emissions are vectored and controlled, they respond in depth to a universal clock or clocking based simultaneously on the speed of the viewer's computer and the speed of the servers and cycles of Second Life itself or themselves. This is in other words, all a setting and background - malleable space governed and governing + and -, as well as malleable time governing +, feed-forward. One can quickly see how functions may be applied across these, for example f(t), $t > 0$, which may or may not get us anywhere; certainly with emissions, for all practical purposes one is reduced to statistical analyses of fuzzy and intersecting (if not interacting) ensembles. So we might say that the digital always moves forwards but spatially may or may not occupy any conceivable confluence, as well as a confluence of the plasma which psychoanalytically is related both to abjection and defuge; in other words, within the human organism at the very least, plasma exhausts and 'ruins' - corrodes, or dissolves, or decays, or corrupts, and so forth. Here the masquerade of the coherency of the subject is called into question as it is in Lacan and elsewhere; here the very exact and astute boundaries that constructed, through code and protocol and software, Second Life itself, are psychologically 'ruined' as well - it's as if one looked at mold and the coding of mold on a molecular level and phenomenologically or culturally tried to conflate the two (which of course is possible but a difficult extension). So in short we might think of the space or spacing within Second Life as a laboratory of sorts, software and hardware (issues of bandwidth and memory internal and external to the viewer and the viewer's computer and connection) in relation to psychological and psychoanalytical issues, again in conjunction with clear or fuzzy considerations of code, the sensorium and the vast but problematic and most likely fictitious masquerading of the regimes of the analog/ic and digit/al themselves.

Eidetic reduction? - impossible, too parasitic, noise. Quietude - gone, emptied space - non-existent. Emptiness, replete, fecund emptiness. The natural attitude - always within reification processes. Too many signs and insufficient generators. To mean is to speak. To speak is to speak among local sound sources; others speaking or listening; overarching sound configuration. Everything is slot or slotted; slots are mobile, futile, fuzzy. Psychoanalytical entities are dispersed from origin; there is no thing seeing, no thing looking or looked at, a theater which is always a mess, never has been anything but a mess - a theater which is under the sign of masquerade or constriction, because it is only with constriction that plot develops, that characters speak, that one lives in the true world, that one inscribes or is inscribes, creates and exhausts meaning, tending always towards abjection, defuge, death, almost in that very order. The blanket origin of death puts an end to it all; it's on the limb or hinge of death that Second Life carries on, and who knows how many are logged in under how many borrowed or originary names?

'Second Life,' miasma

==========================

The object 'Second Life' has sent you a message from Second Life:
Your object 'miasma' has been returned to your inventory lost and found folder from parcel 'Odyssey_ExhibitA_Gallery_zone1' at Odyssey 32.0955, -1.16293 because it went off-world.

= Second Life is owned by (unknown)
= Location unknown.

============================

WRITING MACHINE

A module describes an orbit; particles are emitted at regular intervals. The direction of the particle stream is determined by local 'weather' or 'wind' in second life. The stream is jerked by the orbit, and this results in the repeated generation of similar graphemes or artifacts in the air, which travel along with the stream, slowly disappearing at the farther end. Perhaps this is one source for the sign: something is configured and emitted at regular intervals, the locals stand around and watch.

Julu Twine:

Alan Dojoji has offered you 'aaafloor2' in Second Life. Log in to accept
Alan Dojoji has offered you 'aaaamputee' in Second Life. Log in to accep
Alan Dojoji has offered you '3' in Second Life. Log in to accept or decl
Alan Dojoji has offered you 'maud22' in Second Life. Log in to accept or
Alan Dojoji has offered you 'stripper11' in Second Life. Log in to accep
Alan Dojoji has offered you 'holdingclosee' in Second Life. Log in to ac
Alan Dojoji has offered you 'aaantiparallel3' in Second Life. Log in to
Alan Dojoji has offered you 'aanudance2' in Second Life. Log in to accep
Alan Dojoji has offered you 'aaa' in Second Life. Log in to accept or de
Alan Dojoji has offered you 'aaastrange' in Second Life. Log in to accep
Alan Dojoji has offered you 'thrustext2' in Second Life. Log in to accep
Alan Dojoji has offered you 'thrustext' in Second Life. Log in to accept
Alan Dojoji has offered you 'thrustest' in Second Life. Log in to accept
Alan Dojoji has offered you 'aaafloor1' in Second Life. Log in to accept
Alan Dojoji has offered you 'shortdouble2' in Second Life. Log in to acc
Alan Dojoji has offered you 'shortextended1' in Second Life. Log in to a
Alan Dojoji has offered you 'shorttangent2' in Second Life. Log in to ac
Alan Dojoji has offered you 'aaaacrazy' in Second Life. Log in to accept
Alan Dojoji has offered you 'twotwo' in Second Life. Log in to accept or
Alan Dojoji has offered you 'three' in Second Life. Log in to accept or
Alan Dojoji has offered you 'four' in Second Life. Log in to accept or d
Alan Dojoji has offered you 'sculpt_2008Jul7_20pm37-7_n002' in Second Li
Alan Dojoji has offered you 'sculpt_2008Jul7_20pm35-16_n001' in Second L
Alan Dojoji has offered you 'curl9' in Second Life. Log in to accept or
Alan Dojoji has offered you 'curl7' in Second Life. Log in to accept or
Alan Dojoji has offered you 'curl8' in Second Life. Log in to accept or
Alan Dojoji has offered you 'curla' in Second Life. Log in to accept or

Second Life come visit!

Unique visitors today = 8, yesterday 9, total 143
Peak unique 3, Yesterday 2, Total 10
view all chat "/superg visitors" next greeter.
13, 156
16, 172
7, 179
135
10, 118
126
17, 40, 85
4, 5, 94
1, 99
=2Eeditor a:visited {color: #551A8B}
187
12, 199
206
218
225
232
248
261
25, 286
20, 306

Absence of Light, images and theory

The black images, Second Life, absent of air, absent of light. To make a primitive semiotics: what's black is _not-there, bot-air._

There are two classes of black objects:

1. Architectural. These are interior building parts or prims that ordinarily would lend support and protection for a structure. Here they are always decorative, placed for the participant's sense of well-being.

1a.. Architectural exceptions. These are building parts that cannot be changed because of unavailable permissions or building parts that lead into the structure, which have their own interior/exterior, water/air/ground semiotics.

2. Mobile objects. These are moving objects transformed into silhouettes with unknown convoluted interiors and planar surfaces. They are invades wishing to remain unknown; the move in strangled or stuttered orbits.

2a. Exceptions. At least one moving object is a video surface, and remains visible. There are a number of invisible objects immediately inside and outside the front of the structure which are also video surfaces. There is a binary rotating group consisting of a female-in-motion-capture and a male satellite objects paneled with male organs; the two visually lock after an untold number of revolutions. This sits central on the gallery floor and references the 'mudpile' object near the entrance, which is also circular and low and is textured with the skin of a female Poser avatar. The mudpile is also a video surface as is the complex 'curtain object' hanging above the binary rotating group.

Schelling Hegel in addition to Gongsun Long, Wittgenstein, Carneades

1. At night all cows are black.

2. Identity as concept or image or word is self-contradiction.

3. Nothing is identical to itself.

4. A white horse is not a horse.

5. It is dark, a long object, snake or rope, is in a cave. What do I do. What is the phenomenology.

6. Perhaps it is a white horse.

7. I would feel the texture of the air and the dim glow from the moonlight reveals all.

8. Perhaps it is a cow.

9. At night all things are black; who is to tell a cow from a white horse. I feel the texture of the air and dim glow.

10. I see an absence of light defined only by a visible edge. As an object moves, the visible edge is transformed; if one thinks of the absence as a two-dimensional bounded plane, the transformation of the visible edge implies either an internal complex apparatus or one or more additional dimensions and axes of rotation.

11. As objects absences of light relate phenomenologically to dark matter, everything untoward, nothing appearing, nothing apparent, but effect.

12. Absence of light is the fundamental stratum of Second Life which only appears when summoned, like a golem; its visibility is monitor-dependent, and its fundamental ontology is that of bits and bytes, codes and protocols, computer programs and languages. What appears around or outside the absence of light is uncanny, self-thwarting, hardly an existence at all.

13. The limits of my language are the limits of my world - from the outside looking as language imposes its own semiosis, its structure always already borrowed from the exterior, invisible to most; language in this metaphoric sense is an absence, parole is just talking about things (as ordinary school arithmetic without Godel, Skolem, Tarski, Church is just counting 'them'). What's interior is analytic, what's exterior is sublime, on the way to phenomenology.

14. Absence of light regions occlude one another, passage is difficult, often impossible, we're unused to regions without internal boundaries or names, without meaning, with their spatiality defined only by their surrounds. At Second Life you may navigate these; in first life or real life or that part of the true world somewhere somewhen elsewise than digital culture or artifacts, the fecundity of the world relegates these to the utmost periphery; think of dust-motes, dark corners, worlds beneath floor-boards, uncanny ghosts, and somewhere in the corner of the corner, a monitor still on, however feebly, something moving on the screen, no one looking anywhere. ...

flatblack imaginary

flatblack which is absence determined by video surfacing, coating, video membrane, salve, video cortisone, video of the stuttered shuddered tiling, sputtered or shattered video, splattered video or video spew:

you can really find your way around here
several thousand equivalent images

rounds

yes, well it's possible to take a ride on these things, you might go somewhere perhaps in the best circles, Julu's sloughing hir skin again, she's doing it for anyone, you can't catch it, it disappears, there's always another, you're in the middle of the stream, you can step in it twice, you can step in it more than twice, you can repeat yourself, you can repeat yourself exactly, can't you. so you might take a ride, one shadow to another, let's call them shades, slightly more accurate, forms of ghost-traps, they'll bring you in, you'll emerge with nothing though, hardly a memory, something on the order of repetition-compulsion, perhaps osmosis. life is one skin after another, they're all the same, they all appear the same, something different perhaps to the utmost, but a kind of mechanical equivalence, they're not identical, pseudo-random calculations ensure that, however close one might think of them as such. there's a cliff between the random and the pseudo-random, and that cliff is perception. make no mistake about them = make no mistake about them, nothing goes forever, the Net is fragile, tenuous, at best; it's always about to collapse, it's about collapse. here's where death comes into play: what's about collapse stays on the side of collapse, not death, which is a word and I will stop that when I die, until then, round and round

(From summary.)

6 Second Life:
a. Five month residency in Odyssey, continuous changes almost on a daily basis. (Thanks to Sugar Seville, Gazia Babeli, Ian Ah.)
b. Thinking of SL as malleable space or 'liquid architecture' - creating environments impossible and inconceivable in a real physical world.
i. Entanglement and invisible objects.
ii. Mappings of video and audio on invisible objects.
iii. Shadow-objects which coalesce.
iv. Objects playing with womb-like enclosures, continuous particle generation.
c. Performances from the Biovision Hierarchy (bvh) files from motion capture equipment, inconceivable/untoward/wayward/contrary gestures and behaviors.
i. Behavior collision.
ii. Obtrusive or obsructive behavior.
d. Phenomenology of lived body in untoward spaces.
i. Broken or stuttered spaces
ii. Spaces that remap themselves.
d. Spaces of abjection, dis/ease, discomfort.
i. Texture-mapping from 'real' bodies.
ii. Spaces 'veering' the subject.
iii. Spaces driving the subject's bandwidth/CPU to the limit.
iv. Spaces driving the subject's ability to walk/fly hir avatar to the limit.

bicorporeal sexuality of architecture

[8:49] 2008) : like (Saved I said Julu - 22 you 22:32:33 can 2008) do like [8:49] I : said (Saved - you Julu can 22 do 22:32:33 whatever Julu want 22:33:16 22:33:16 you but [8:49] think (Saved if what space to on acheive constrained is - a the space better that what on want constrained to the is better a way the may sky be [8:49] make (Saved up 22 in way sky be 22:34:41 way i have have and used 22:34:41 gallery i context, like and the altered to it, just just it, away if with what it's want box I 22:35:09 sky help (Saved need, the set the teleport if from you skybox sounds [8:50] - The this sounds directly great above this [8:50] directly The above skybox space? not Sexual - Life: message User will not be online the message space? will [8:50] stored There delivered a later. couple [8:51] more There I are want couple and more delivered things later. gallery, and which hopefully take will few do days in hopefully gallery, people which come Life: explore User [8:52] all all delivered prims [8:52] black : video to surfaced, make 'sexually and textured' I so like whole womb. thing [8:52] appears Sexual womb. not [8:53] - also will rewrote be script, now which, deliberate) by bounces accident a (but prim now out deliberate) of bounces a prim which, out by of accident reach if when you anyone stand comes where near it stand when where anyone it comes was near send into down air; below I'm floor to or make into send air; down I'm below going the 'ceiling' to invisible that, that, the most sexually likely 'ceiling' sexually prims textured would work? be So sometime would and sometime you next textured week work? thank the greatly! not you I can said do - you think [8:49] whatever : you (Saved want [8:49] Julu : 22 (Saved 2008) Julu think 2008) if but want better is a the on better constrained to way a be space to the space like 22:34:41 way i gallery have context, used and the it, it's but better if altered what it, do is it's away make help sky to help 2008) with gallery that to and if up and skybox [8:50] directly can above this [8:50] the message not will online things a in will hopefully few people days [8:51] come Sexual explore Life: - User [8:51] not Sexual online Life: stored the delivered black later. stored prims make black all all want 'sexually all textured' the [8:52] like also later. rewrote [8:53] prim deliberate) out bounces of a it you was stand it where of the sexually likely thank next [8:53] stored said said

Experimental Mathesis

Because of the relative mathematical complexity of mapping three-dimensional behavior with motion capture software, the visual results vary widely from filter to filter; as in early crystal radio tuning, there's no smooth differentiable curve as constants and functions slowly change.

There are so many patterns in nature! Beyond the usual simple and complex tilings, there are non-repetitive tilings re: Penrose and others; there are fractal and chaotic regimes as well. We can also mention all sorts of 'monstrous' curves. Given the complexity of human behavior and dynamics, however, I think it's fair to say that the occurrences here at the Virtual Environments Lab are deeply unpredictable; while the filter is relatively rigid and secure (in these cases), the results are tempered with the exigencies of muscles and bones and gravity, as well as creativity, skill, intention, and so forth. A filter can exaggerate, i.e. increase time and space contrast, minute differences, but it can also diminish them to the extent that a kind of collapse occurs - the limit of course being 0, reducing everything to equivalent quiescence. All of this is fundamental and basic to the calculus; one might metaphorically consider what's happening in these videos as a _double movement,_ of human behavior in the first place, and shape-riding in the second. And how far must one go through the process, only to return again to the semblance of organic life? And what is the point of the journey, involving code and protocols, the real and the virtual, concrete substance, organic metabolism and mobility, as well as an overriding abstraction and impulse to re/produce something elsewhere that is once more identifiable within the comfort zone of lived experience?

These videos/stills always surprise, always seem to offer something to be studied, from perception to a language of perceiving, and from the habitus of deeply lived environment to insistent anomalies in dialectic with problematic and overarching form.

Games and Cowers

The new scripts construct a game from SL exhibition space; fly through (see gamethrobs.mov) and objects disappear for twenty seconds - how much of the space can you clear? In the meantime clutter and new video reconstruct the space, Julu (see cower jpgs) has a new look and powers, and hysteria pervades prim prims and abject objects. Increasingly the theory's in the doing of the space, the perceiving of it, the flying and walking and running through it. Disappearing prims might send you spiral downward, but there are teleport spheres below to return you to the surface. It's all compact and blown apart ...

Dreams of Better Worlds Concrete

| Images from intractive avatar game in The Accidental Artist exhibition,
| SL; avatar movement deconstructs architecture, frees the space. No
| score, no wins or losses; continuous play produces continuous
| deconstruction. The video is in black and white; color from the site
| refuses to compress properly.

Think of it: Second Life (or similar virtual spaces) as a simulacrum of humanity's dream of flying, of malleable space and time; think of SL as a laboratory for the practical/theoretical phenomenology of space and time. What occurs in human flight, in the presence of strangers, in weight= lessness, in sudden weight, in anonymity, in exposure, in agoraphobia or clausterphobia? I work daily and nightly in the exhibition space, trying things out, not primarily for the aesthetics, but for the cog-sci, psycho- logical, psi-a comprehension that may or may not occur. Lacan or Minsky might not be at home in these spaces, but they exist on the periphery of theory. It's far too easy to dismiss virtual spaces in relation to what might be considered the other, in terms of community, politics, political economy, information economy, religion, etc. But first there is community in SL, ideological struggle, etc., although not played out against the scarcity of necessary resources; bandwidth and prim number are irrelevant compared to lack of food or sleep. On the other hand it's the very absence of noise that makes SL more like a savanna than an urban center, and a savanna that at times allows one to speak and perceive with a clarity bordering on the uncanny. While it may be slightly difficult learning to move smoothly through SL, it's no more difficult than learning a sport or board-game, and the results are equally enriching.

I don't want to sound like an advertisement for SL or virtual worlds in general - but I do want to indicate their potential for psychological and phenomenological experimentation. What one sees can be seen from one's home; there's an established intimacy that the heavy cultural institutionalization of museums and galleries doesn't have. The economy is on a far smaller scale as well; over the years I've been on SL for example,, I've paid eight dollars and eighty cents in real money for uploads to the SL server - a small price, given the potential. Most of what I construct - animations, textures, sounds, texts, prims, are created with open source software outside SL.

To fly, to make objects disappear and appear at will, to revolve or otherwise motivate them, to ignore or stress gravity, to move among the problematic of things, to move through them, to court invisibility, to view oneself from one's body or alterity, to speak or write (courting both phoneme and grapheme), to operate within or beneath erasure, to create or annihilate, send objects into or out of the world - to do any of these things, and more, in any combination - within the limits of the computer - limits which are perhaps far too often emphasized (instead of seeing potential and the potential for expansion) - this is what, for the moment while the net is up and running - this is what we can work with, in however limited our physical off-world conditions might be - and this is the promise, holding for the slightest while - for the premise of communication or its lack, analogic inert and digital coded and their intermingled limits. It continues to surprise me, how many complaints there are about these worlds, from lambda-moo and earlier, and how little joy is expressed over their current possibilities - what they can do _now._ Forget the holodeck; there are already (what would have passed for) miracles afoot. This isn't arguing against the need for deconstruction and critique of SL's and other virtual worlds' political economy - just that one can proceed in addition from the bottom up, seeing for example what happens when a prim is grounded or sent elsewhere, say, into another physics, with a shape-rider upon it, another shape-rider perhaps desperately controlling the action, such as it is.

Then again, what constitutes a prim, a thing, a thing-in-itself, a protocol, a code, an atom, a table of elements or fundamental particles, a resonance or plasma sending material worlds askew, exhausted, towards the defuge of potential (but never complete) annihilation? And what better way to think these things through, than to try them, on however distorted or miniscule a scale. -

Trails

I can see if someone has come into the exhibition space in Second Life; they leave a trail behind them, objects and spews that slowly disappear - in the meantime, the space is oddly denuded.

I want to explain why the space looks like an acid trip, why it's so crowded, so preposterous. And the reason has to do with anti-art, or non-art, making something that construes an environment instead of presenting an object or installation for contemplation. The objects in the SL exhibition have depth; they're not pieces or scatter pieces or process work - they're environment, an environmental space close to useless, replete, fecund. What appears to be actions are trajectories, complex interactive fields that mimic sentience.

Objects and spews head toward the depths; Julu is down there among them, moving in and out of the way, looking for the teleport sphere to return her to the surface. The teleport sphere is a phallic object, contained, curtailed; it is the only sculpture in the neighborhood.

Think of the space, spacings, as an ensemble of interrelated ecological niches; there are local customs, nestings, vectors, behaviors and behavior collisions. The space is utterly transformed through participatory movement that environmental resonates.

It's only this way that complex and alien phenomenologies assert themselves - there's no piece or artwork presenting one or another problematic, only a skein or membrane simultaneously tending towards thought and its absence.

Weather, whether

From above you might or might not have weather, you might or might not stay with the local environment as the Linden gods hand it down - always benign, never too much wind, no rain or snow or sleet or hail, nothing to set your mind anywhere but at ease. No air, textured clouds, mostly cumulus I think, and I think two banks of them. Fog, yes, and a day might cycle through 7-8 hours, I never counted. But you can set eternal time, you can set it at midnight, at dawn or dusk, at midday. You might move the sun around, you might set fog heights or intensities, all in eternal space where avatars live forever, but disappear, and who is to know whether any disappearance is sad and final and prims forever lost. There's no fear but from the servers, as invisible as the furies, and there are no shadows but from the sun and thin light from a moon that seems full always, but who is to know this as well, or any thing within a space that seems controlled and dire; you might float or fly, but your world is bounded, inescapable, even with small holes of video, live or otherwise, small holes of sound, live or otherwise. Nothing is going to come out and touch you, not now, and soon in the future, when the hand reaches from the screen, who knows what force or thing or organism is driving it, who knows what intention lies behind it, what danger lurks. We live in ignorance within and without, and that only for that short time beyond which an utter inconceivable blankness reigns. You can control lights, but local lights rarely make shadows, and even that, everything, depends on bandwidth and bandwidth settings, on frames and frame-rates, on complexity of prims and texture sizes, on the number of participants online at any moment - all sorts of things you might well study and examine, viewing the stats bars, coming on later and later at night as others disappear elsewhere, without a murmur and only the slightest increase of speed. You know you're riding on the dead, on silent computers, on all those lives logged off now and then or permanently, and who is to know, who is to know, who is to know.

ii. If this transmission is not dev/nul and void, it will reach you. If it does not reach you, I write under a differend configured by the Net and its political economy. If I protest on the occasion of fog, you will not hear me. If you are my enemy and have passed on, you may have died, you may be elsewhere, you may be off the grid, you may be on another. If you are my enemy, your silence unnerves me; if you are my friend, your presence is an unknown sign, just as absence can be of any thing or any one, and zero may carry 0*X, insofar as X is finite, and regular, normative, and then who knows?

In the fog of Second Life, preferences also govern distance - what can or cannot be seen out there - what constitutes the Pale. Enter the Pale and familiarity twists and perhaps disappears; go far enough, and you may be grieving for another home, griefing among aliens. Within your space, however, you are comforted, surrounded by familiar objects, you may have constructed these objects, they are history for you, they refuse decay, they may escape out of world, but are always there as if gleaming and presenced, and shininess is something else again that may or may not be turned out, permitted, just as in the real world where sun and shininess are everywhere presencing. But here it is not the local light, at least not in my version; in my version my home is on an island and there are hills and clouds, and what's beyond, Heere bee Dragonnes, is unknown, as I have been saying, and perhaps even unaccountable and unaccounted-for. I inhabit a great and jagged sphere and move comfortably, and in the distance there is that smoothness, that fog that is always present, always there, day or night, that fog against which all things comfortable and local are measured, my home in the midst of the fog, my neighbors, my friends ...

Alone

Julu: I'm trying to tell you something, my gums
bleed, corrode, just like any others, in this stillness air,
in this absent air.
Nikuko: Wind blowing through you, around you, we
wait for those moments when sound will penetrate
bodies, resonate with dim and elder woods,
make noise and even music, among us, to our delight.

Julu: In these dark woods, lights are pasted
across our sheave-skin bodies, blinding us;
through pure absence, nothing happens, codes are processed,
roil within the distant machines, at times no further
than the kindly things at home.
Nikuko: Speculating beyond your means, but yet my powers
have grown into astonishing beliefs. I can move things
I no longer can caress; the real flees from me, I am left
distraught, along in spaces emptied of abstract surfaces.
Julu: At a distance, we touch, and no longer no closer;
our loneliness lies in our uselessness for approach, caress,
and love. We meld into each other sometimes bridged across
these spaces, leaving trails and vestiges of garnered
presence - notes across chasms, worlds tuned across voids
where we, alien and aligned, despair of ever talking.
Nikuko: Yet born of one another, borne among each other,
our love continues to build, tune and emulate, and emulate
again, until nothing of original remains, only physics
born of inconceivable signs 'raised to an incandescent power.'
Julu: What is cleared, of space and time, is always replete;
what is replete is always alone; our things are never
in-themselves, but among-others; our monads slur their
boundaries helplessly, we are at the mercy of things and gods,
machines far beyond control.
Nikuko: Our love is always memory, that is our love.
Julu: Our flights, our poise, our wandering ways.
Nikuko: Prayerful life is useless, only our deaths entwined
will save us. -

tantric space

Tantric eyes are everywhere
Avatar legions come and stare
Slowly spaces turn up cleared
It's what objects have always feared
Open holes often leered
leads cross other places
When you go leave your traces
Your sight is buried in sites
You set world to days or nights
Objects murmur with fearful glows
Light sound make wayward shows
Across the floors their numbers legion
Crossing another region
Video grinds worlds halt
just a momentary bandwidth fault
touch ball below

again return flow
As if body spews drains
Against boundaries where it rains
The smoke spells out uncanny words
Prims disappear like frightened herds
Come forward get tantric due
Cum frantic dew
What see hardly leisure
Present for hardened pleasure
Leave all this empty behind
time place mind
worl ays soun waywar an
eo grins worls s Vi
banwilt's ban
wi
th y bo
isappear frightene hir hersforwar ueewharenePresent har
ene behinLeave behinmin

Tantric eyes are everywhere
Avatar legions come and stare
Slowly spaces turn up cleared
It's what objects have always feared
Open holes are often leered
Open leads cross other places
When you go you leave your traces
Your sight is buried in other sites
You set your world to days or nights
Objects murmur with fearful glows
Light and sound make wayward shows
Across the floors their numbers legion
Crossing to another region
Video grinds the worlds to halt
It's just a momentary bandwidth fault
You touch your ball and go below
You touch again return and flow
As if your body spews and drains
Against the boundaries where it rains
The smoke spells out uncanny words
Prims disappear like frightened herds
Come forward get your tantric due
Cum forward set your frantic dew
What you see is hardly leisure
Present for your hardened pleasure
Leave all this empty world behind
Leave time and place and leave your mind

How to move through the exhibition space at Odyssey fun

This presumes you have downloaded the software, which installs itself automatically; after that, use the URL below and then read on.

If you go to view the Odyssey exhibition, try tuning the interface; it works best if you set the time at midnight through the Environment Settings in the World directory of the menu. If you use the environmental editor, you can set the atmosphere/image at Pirate and increase the mist. If you use ctl-alt-t, you can see invisible objects (perhaps). If you begin the video, and it ends as you move through the space, start it again; there is different video in different parts of the space, and the same goes for the audio - except for the 12 small invisible audio cubes. If it's running slow, open the menu, go to Edit/Preferences/Graphics and lower the Quality and Performance. You may also check Custom, then check Atmospheric Shaders. When you enter the space, try flying through objects; they will move out of the way for the most part, for between 10 and 30 seconds. Fly and turn around and you'll see you've cleared a space. If you see a sphere, you may touch it with a left-hand mouse click; a sphere above takes you below, and vice versa. The spheres don't move out of the way. If you walk through the space, try going between the stairs into the water below, or fall through the well, or go over the wall bounding the island. You may not be able to take your avatar there; click on View and then on Camera Controls; you'll see a small panel open. The controls on the right slide your viewpoint left or right, up or down; the middle slides it in or out, and the left turns it about various axes. You can use this to look beneath the surface of the water where the avatar won't go, or to slide into the space in order to see the objects without having them disappear in the presence of the avatar. You can zoom in on the objects or enter into the particle streams and watch them fill the screen with objects and color. You can go through the floorboards with the Camera Control and see the objects that have disappeared from the surface. If you go to the right of the building wall, you'll notice dark figures disappearing on occasion into the distance - these are avatar emanations from the objects and appear every once in the while, perhaps 10 to 20 seconds themselves. You may sit on some of the objects by right-clicking the mouse button on them, then clicking on Sit Here - sometimes it's possible, and sometimes not. You may be able to sit on a moving object which gives you a local ride. If you type 'm' or use the menu, you may active the Mouselook function which allows you to see the world 'through' the avatar's eyes, and this is fine for a ride or exploration. You don't have access to Camera Control in Mouselook. With some moving objects, you may be able to go beneath them when they rise; they might push you down through the floor to the water below, where you will use the sphere to return. You may also be cast into the air or find yourself tripping or you may find yourself pushed out of the way. If other people, avatars, are in the space, you may talk and chat with them; if you rise above the space, you can watch them as objects disappear in their vicinity, and space is cleared for them and for your view from above. You may want to look for a moment at the site at dawn or dusk, which adds lovely reds or pinks, and you can activate these through the Environment editor as well; midday is the least interesting. If you want to take a digital image or photograph of the scene, you can use the Snapshot function at the bottom of the screen, or Take Snapshot, ctl-shift-s, under the File menu; the advantage of the latter is that you can tune the direction your avatar is looking by moving the panel around on the screen before taking the shot. You may use ctl-r to run through the space, which takes objects out faster. You may find it difficult to enter or leave the space - there are invisible barriers built into the gamespace itself, and it is easiest to enter to the right of the announcement sign; if you have difficulty navigating you can always fly into the space and then walk around or continue flying. If you have the talk function enabled on the lower right of your screen, and a microphone, you can talk to other avatars or make noise, and if you have speakers you can of course listen to other avatars talking as well. Chances are you will be alone or with one or two people at a time in the environment, but this allows you to explore the objects fully without having them disappear as the result of other avatars' movements. Below are some images from the current state of the installation, which is at a kind of 'plateau,' and won't change for the next few days.

Weight

anomalies of recognition between weighted object and Julu Twine
s/he buries hir head in the sand
s/he recovers and that complicates matters of representation

the weighted object has pushed Julu Twine down into the sand
s/he is standing in and out of the sand and the ground deconstructs
by which Julu means that the ground is opened and oddly angled
and that the ground is not at gamespace's edge

Second Life as a lab - continues to be a lab. how long before this set of constraints, images, geographies, bandwidths and game engine, becomes stale, bulky, close to collapse. I will close my eyes, says Julu, and the same things reign near & far, surely there is more to life than this, signifiers of defuge handed down by their creator Linden Labs and whatever whomever the associates. I will close my eyes and will hear nothing more. Nikuko says, I hear nothing more. chorus, that our space is tawdry in eptitude and plenitude, close to the starved prim, all sheave-skins are alike, equivalent. chorus, it takes few rules to deceive the eye and its rule, few rules for sight and sound. Julu, I will continue to dwell, this defuge itself is sufficient, this disgust, this paste. for if it were not for this, what might emerge is (would be within) the range and reign of the digital, now here is something different, this paste, exhaustion, limitation. chorus, the rings no long sound their particle home. Nikuko, the rings have absented, where are they, what fecundity has driven them away, elsewhere. Julu, not elsewhere but absent-in-depth, that is to say a mode not working stillborn, that is to say the scripting has returned to dead language, that is to say nothing to perform here in these parts. chorus, that is to say already performed or sounded, sighted, rendered useless by a constant. Julu, the constant of the game. Nikuko, the constant of Linden Labs, nothing that is arbitrary or sloughed off. Julu, nothing skimmed or spewed. Nikuko, nothing that derides-derails the protocol. Julu, code-coding performance. chorus, who knows what we will do. Nikuko, in response. Julu, in response. chorus, but within, not without. chorus but within the sloughed, circumscribed the slough. Nikuko, but in response. Julu, but in response.

My not inconsiderable sins in Second Life

I have overburdened the servers with far too many video and image textures.
I have added too many prim scripts to too many objects.
I have required far to complex screen redrawings time and time again.
I have taken apart the building where the exhibition is held.
I have revolved the panels of the building eternally and they may jump as well from place to place.
I have dissolved the boundaries of the building and opened it to every aspect of the environment.
I have sent particles onto foreign soil or the soil of other parcels.
I have created problematic images to texture both prims and particles.
I have clotted the environment with particles and immoderate prims.
I have created circulations among particles and prims that threaten to subvert the intentions of other artists or cultural workers anywhere in the vicinity.
I have made it difficult to enter or leave the exhibition.
I have made it quite possible to trap the viewer beneath the floor of the exhibition until a gateway sphere is round.
I have coated gateway spheres and other objects from time to time with obscene or sexual imagery.
I have created a false sense of tantric enlightenment by the completion and generation stages of gods unknown to me.
I have betrayed the trust of those who fly and those who walk or run into the complex of the exhibition space.
I have made the organized disorganized and the countable uncountable and unaccounted-for.
I have created a sense of disequilibrium and non-equilibrium thermodynamics in a space known for the excellence of its organization and propriety of its codes and protocols.
I have brought a sense of miasma and sleaziness into the perfection of parameter and prim.
I have opened the exhibition space to the effects and influences of places and spaces outside the structure proper and opened places and spaces outside the structure to the effects and influences of the exhibition space.
I have blurred the distinction between internal and external.

I have created an environment close to that considered griefing along with grieving and griefing avatars that seem self-contained and somewhat intimidating to those unfamiliar with the operations and customs of Second Life.
I have placed far too much information in far too small a space and time making it impossible to grasp or digest the subtleties of the exhibition which most likely will be overlooked.
I have taxed administrators and programmers alike in the daily reorganization and reconfiguration of the space.
I have returned objects and avatars to other spaces.
I have sent objects out of world and some of them have never been returned.
I have created and reveled in a mess where others might want at least a modicum of order in order to comprehend the mass aesthetics that seems to constitute a very problematic work.
I have overlaid the whole with far too much theory.
I have thought too much and have left little space for spontaneous creation with the exception of the tunings and retunings that constantly occur.

Ideal Unaccountable Space

IDEAL: Black anomalous SPACE. The light SOURCE is EITHER interior GLOW, defined by the OBJECTS THEMSELVES, or external ATMOSPHERIC LIGHT from SUN or MOON. Or NONE OF THESE. The SPACE is SELF-DEFINING, apparently BOUND- LESS, within which INORDINATE OBJECTS define themselves. GRAVITY has been SET to CONTROL two WITHIN such; these are CONTRARY to the MEANS and WAYS of LITTORAL REVOLUTION.

This isn't anything that could be done outside of Second Life, and giving an experience otherwise than being.

Hi Sugar, an open letter which is also a text or poetics -

This is the fallingsky series, which occurs in the skysphere; it needs the base exhibition space to make any sense, I think. There are several elements in it, including physical objects which collide and may in fact go out of world, leave the lifespace altogether. That's fine with me; it's always possible to replenish them. There are other objects that rotate, and objects that both rotate and shuttle; these are a form of creative impulse. At small volume, shuttle turns to shudder, frisson, as if there were an organism within that adjusts itself homeostatically every decade of seconds or so. The organisms - those with weight, those which rotate, those which shuttle, interpenetrate and interact with one another; nothing is produced but the semblance of community, which for all intents and purposes _is_ community. Another element is a small rotating lozenge which generates the usual rings; these are small textures sufficiently light to run on most machines with everything else going. Here, the element clearly shuttles in a rectangular pattern which is reproduced as a lineage; this is evident in the shuttled rectangles strung out along the ring-beads which of course are particles in constant but relatively even movement. All of these objects and spews, and murmurs of movement, deconstruct the machine, any such, reconstructing organism out of the remnants, or at least the dream or miasma of organism. It fascinates me that the show here in the skysphere has to be constantly tended, to keep the objects within.

The sexuality of these objects is one of apparent infinite or wrapped pattern - a sexuality which transverses fields which are self-defining; in other words the transversing is both field and transversal, transgression and ingression. Thus the textures, mouths, lozenges, against an infinite blackness that wraps upon itself with the thinnest of shells.

Here, within the skysphere, I find I can work with almost total freedom, without restraint from gravity - unless desired - and other artifacts coding and reminiscent of the real/physical world both within virtual and physical space, what I call the true real. So just as my stay at West Virginia is coming to an end, so the space has become the most fully developed I'm capable of at the moment. Since I have, I think, several months of residency left (three?), I can use this arena or space as a crucible for viewing and re/viewing phenomenological issues of objects and their potential inconceivability. Don't forget that even ordinary objects won't last very long in the grand scheme of things - a scheme in which plasma, not hardened material substances - is the dis/order of the day. For me, _every_ object is inconceivable, both intrinsically and extrinsically, and this crucible, skysphere, gives me the opportunity to explore these issues - particularly as the entrance to the sphere should be through the already existing Odyssey exhibition space proper. Just as there are teleport spheres sending one down into the water and/or out again, so there should be teleport spheres sending one up as if indefinitely into the skysphere. The semiotics of the skysphere are set out in the exhibition, which can be read as a moving and perhaps virulent book; this coding basis, appearing as a self-generating field of part-objects, then infuses the demateriality of the skysphere. The skysphere itself is non-text, and its contents non-textual; there are residues and residences of the uncanny and abject present, as well as negation, homeostasis, and intermittency.

(Beginning of problematic claim.) All of this above isn't about Second Life itself, although manifestations like the skysphere would be different elsewhere. It's also not about Linden Labs, current server costs, bandwidth issues, game computers and the like; these will change and the political economy of the Net will continue to transform (if not disappear altogether). Right or wrong, I think of this work as concerned with the phenomenology of the virtual, and the inhering of the virtual in the physical world. This inhering has existed since dreams, gestures, languagings, tools, customs, have existed - in other words, since culture has existed, and one can easily make a case that culture has existed all the way down; even amoeba demonstrate learning and adaptation. The phenomenology of the virtual is about our very being, our inhabiting, of ourselves, others, worlds, signs, totalities and their ruptures. It's interesting to think of _this_ virtual world at this time as a practical laboratory for philosophical work, but I claim that it is, and that this and other spaces create unique opportunities for participant-observation in epistemological, ontological, and other issues, often considered off-limits to concrete experimental investigaton. (End of problematic claim.)

Please let me know how to activate a teleport sphere to these regions; is a flight bracelet required or desired? And let's do an announcement to open it up to a public, if possible. In the meantime, there's always the fallingsky jpg series, as well as a very short video segment indicating blackness and blurred potential.

Inside the Sphere, description and theory

Several molecular engines within the aegis of the sphere; out of world anomalous behavior seems to have slowed. I'm running Second Life on my Asus eeepc 701; contrary to what I've read, the installation went in flawlessly and SL runs reasonably well in the Debian Etch environment. I made a few minor changes, placing the cache on an external flash card for example; the SL client wouldn't run from the card, but the cache is fine. To make up for the 512 meg memory, I increased the cache to 600 meg and turned media off. Everything runs, albeit slowly; the image is clear enough to allow some house-cleaning on the road.

Inside the sphere, since it's self-contained - an 'environment' seems to form, one that appears self-bounded. In other words, there is always inscription; if it's not inherent in a given virtual world, it's going to be created as soon as one begins to configure anything. An object carries structure; even anomalous or ghostly spews or objects create an uncanny domain (appear to tap an uncanny domain).

In other words, inside the sphere, you don't see the sphere, flat black against nothing. So the objects are there, but you don't necessarily think they're _somewhere._ Where they are is circumscribed by their presence. They seem to be a closed manifold. There doesn't seem to be anything beyond them. The manifold seems differentiable. The ring streams, though, seem to go somewhere; they're vectors, directed line segments; they seem cut off; they disappear; perhaps there's something to that disappearance, after all. One moves around and among objects and rings and whatever one might consider particles and objects, but it's difficult to move around here without breaking the fragility of the illusion, what might be considered a second-order illusion.

What's presenced within the sphere, a simulacrum of an organism, simultaneously passive and generating; the repetition of a rectangle defined only as a process (again, a second-order process within the processes/protocols of Second Life itself), moving and disappearing, clearly the result of an other movement drawing and drawn in three- dimensional space; a signal or memory of a signal: A memory of a signal is a signal; a signal is always memory. How clear that is in the sphere! How clearly understood!

And such is the meaning-memory of organism and the murmuring of organism, even in a digital-granular domain such as this one.

of death and dealing

preparatory moves, logging in through the cache. this is the background of gamespace memory; in 3 and 1 for example you can see the fundamental prims on the way to full load. the full grey is on the way to skysphere. resolution is lower but higher than you might imagine; one can sacrifice speed and framerate for resolution.

this is the reverse processing of worlds after death, as full a representation as one might want of bardo, which is unrepresentable. one emerges out of nothing, returns to it through a world always already emptied and empty.

death

there are no dealings with death
death doesn't deal with you
you don't see the hands of death
death doesn't show its cards

death shows its cards to the living
sometimes they weep and wail
the casket doesn't exist
ashes and body don't exist

death's cards are never stacked
there is no stacking the cards
there are no cards of death
there's no dealing with the living

there's no understanding the living
they walk around and talk
they stutter stumble shudder
the other stops them

the other is their body
the other is their death's body
death doesn't exist
the other doesn't either

julu murmured hello
julu, no, s/he
nikuko muttered i couldn't care less
but not murmured. something else, closer to muttering, friendlier.
not whispering, nothing like that.
but not i couldn't care less. something else, closer to disdain,
but not quite. a return that veered into the unknown. but polite,
polite conversation, not exactly a rejoinder. nikuko muttering,
i thought so, or i thought you knew. an implication, knowing:
more than that, more than you'd let on. but not that exactly.
julu, murmuring - hello.
nikuko, muttering - it could only get worse.
or it will only get worse. but what, a morning, afternoon, or
evening. or somewhere else, perhaps it will turn elsewhere,
against the odds. as if julu garbled. perhaps these two fine
people. but it falls off, these weren't the volleys or returns.
these weren't anything at all. 'all memories are memories of
annihilation.' that's it, for what could be remember if there
were no end to it, packaging, however brief and quickening.
nikuko, muttering: there's an end to an end, call it memory.
julu, murmuring: i remember now, hello again.

exile

i can't believe where it's gotten me again. this exile, this denudation, this exhaustion which seeps through me like the Caucasus. burned, i would do no less than refuse the laws of gravity, gravitas, hopeful instead that one might finally fly elsewhere, elsewhen.whatever the case was, it wasn't mine. there was an explosive within, expulsion of air, breath gone awry. this was remonstrance imminent: nothing lasts where the only sense of origin is rooted in the body, your body, inherent in it, inhering. place it in the mouth or eyes, place it in the cunt. you can't leave without magic, there are no signposts, nothing, nowhere to go. not when you're a planet yourself, among self and selves.honor the dead is no honor at all, you are in the breathless realm, beings depend on you.

you have to follow the realm of the dead, travel beneath the surface, hurtle into the skysphere, which more often than not may reject you, try and again until you're there. what is flat back recreates your Origin within you; fecundity has no presence. see how poor these video remnants are; travel yourself with yourself, your Origin, and see exactly that, process and operators, self-generations, completions and then some

After this I needed air.

The jumble begins to take advantage of screen resolution and frame/flicker rate; objects revolve and generate lissajous/moire/illusory patterns as a result of hatchings and cross-hatchings, read/write speed, cache speed, and a host of other variables.Jumble changes from machine to machine, resolution to resolution, and shading operators. Moving through the space, turning video/sound on and off - the phenomenology changes in relation to the dialectic established when an abacus was first used, at lightning speed, bullae scattered everywhere. Every marker is always already virtual, every marker is on the way towards disappearance, every annihilation has the potential for memory, perhaps later, inscription. The jumble here resolves, as every jumble does, on a micro-level; it is the non-aristotelian that throws everything off, gesture which trips up where raster and orthogonal configurations lie.

Jumble in physical reality = noisy, not chaotic. Jumble in Second Life = equivalent to the order of perfection = the perfection of order.

flix

another attempt obviating moire/lissajous. site passed Vegas a while ago:

site has no weight, thin slice; what the screen does, inertial mass, something else, carrier or parasite. it all disappears shortly after death. I need someone creating hardware, stone, nonexistent inscriptive bulwark. Julu cries out of Titus Andronicus, will be forgotten. words lose tongues and hands, painlessly, but extrinsic, unable to testify. no testimony, no annihilation; successful annihilation is no annihilation at all. memory relies on death, diacritical-death, as if something were amiss. tongues and hands are painful; Second Life, airless, disappears among them. Waking this morning I realized this work is unbelievably flimsy, fragile, entirely disappearing at the end of the residency - a radical disassembly that hardly passes for erasure - given that nothing existed here in the first place. This absence becomes an unreadable epitaph under erasure. These words, too owe their existence to the imminence of electrical charges far and beyond that of paper, stone, scissors, rock. So it goes and doesn't return.

moss

moss textures from the atoll package.
moss is neither volume nor surface; maximal and exquisite, fondling earth or bark or stone, it portends maternal fecundity, Julu Twine murmuring in her sleep.
moss is temperate, comforting, meandering lazily among ants and lichen.
so many microbes, so much going on, in a pillow of soft and entrancing moss!
moss in air, tendrils floating, almost, but not quite, hanging.
moss of mist, mist-moss, the very depth of organism!
neither object nor clothing surface lovely Julu Twine!
Julu Twine inhabits moss creatures, lichen, air-plankton creatures, misted, glowing, submerged, subterranean, in the midst of quiet winds.
moss softens what was hard, blurs what was defined, obscures what was clear, colors what was transparent, warms what was cool, hugs and delights in stone and earth, embraces bark - yes, mist-creatures, the slightest of fogs.
moss is always an ellipsis, speaking of moss is memory of moss.
even in front of one, moss is a memory, close to disappearance, evanescent.close to disappearance, closed to disappearance.
moss is open and closed, closed and open - look, it's almost forgotten!
the sward, mobile and translucent; Julu says more organism! more organism!
Julu Twine separates hirself from moss and memory, lichen and bark, air and water and earth. But moss separates itself as well; equivalence tunnels through equivalence; moss and Julu Twine emerge; here's where inscription starts and falters!

nukie

Julu Twine wears my skin which goes to magic places, penetrations by armies and young maiden youths, milky streams, mossed rocks, spheres with no landing, manifolds with no surface for a calm and lovely sitting - Julu Twine wears my skin, wears me, hir scent inflames, expands my slivered organ replete with carved inscription, how useless:Her skins lost in moss or plans of fabrication, hir skins coming foward, damped and suffused, hir skins of warmer weathers, hir skins of suckling cocks, hir skins of flowed interiors, such membranes, tissues, of organism s/he speaks, drools of sex caught, cauterized:Julu Twine is present, supple and impossible skin, such pubescent glow, slight swellings everywhere, all surfaces, interiors, scent among asymptotic spheres, what glows moves into body, twined of the flames, cool and aroused::

Your my heroin, caffeine, serotonin, miasma, cocaine, hash, alcohol, strychnine, absinthe, mercury... is in-me my where

heroin, caffeine, serotonin, miasma, cocaine, hash, alcohol, strychnine, absinthe, mercury...

Your impossible connects my heroin, caffeine, serotonin, miasma, cocaine, hash, alcohol, strychnine, absinthe, mercury... with needle

park

srenilyc dna snoitcennoc fo stsehc::.llew sa sevael ,flesti tcejbo eht
,noitatic eht dna etis eht evael i ;nrob-llits si gnihtyreve tub .emit ni
tniop siht ta lacitirc smees taht ygolopot ot yhpargopot morf evom a -
cinagro eht ro cinihcam eht rehtie fo ecalp ni tros niatrec a fo
ytivitcennoc stneserp tsael ta hcihw ',ratava' dna ',edon' ',rednilyc'
sretcarahc htiw gnitirw neeb ev'i .elpoep eht wonk neve t'nod i dna
noisivelet no seispotua fo spuesolc era ereht ,doog t'nsi ereh dnuora swen
eht .uoy ot kcits a dloh t'nac taht seidob ratava htiw ysub oot neeb ev'i
refinnej uoy togrof i:.regnuh ,htaed ,tsud ,snoteleks ,senob ,tsap eht fo
xedni etaciled siht ,ti dnuof i nehw deirc i ho - detnuah ,esaeler
,derehtetnu ,etacifitrec taht evah i ;tirem fo etacifitrec a dedrawa saw
enoemos 1481 ni .etag eht ta retlaf sgnitirw ym os tsuj - sdlrow fo
ytiligarf eht fo ,siht fo dias eb nac tahw .kcabdeef ,ecnalab laropmet ot
deit os ,eligarf os er'yeht - snoitatneserper fo nieks a ni dezinagro era
skrow dna sgnignoleb ym lla .syad fo rettam eht ni ,ylkciuq deneppah hcihw
noisrepsid a ,sedaced revo delbmessa dna dezinagro ehs dlrow eht fo
noisrepsid eht :htaed yna ni sneppah tahw ,deid rehtom ym nehw dnahtsrif
denrael i ;meht evah t'nod netfo dna seman deen sgniht .msinagro dna
noitcennoc fo egrem eht si rewolf eht ,epahs a si rewolf eht ,dnucef
,detcennoc si rewolf eht:.dlrow eht krow .meht tegrof .emit ni tniop siht
ta yrassecen ylno sporp ynam os sa raeppasid taht stcurtsnoc cinihcam
,slexip ,smirp tub gnihton .nrobhtrae ,nrobria ,htriber fo etats tnatsnoc
ni ,sselriah ,desnaelc ,lautriv eht fo yranigami ,laer eht fo tirg eht
,noitatneserper fo seihpargopot ,aidem fo seigolopot ,aidem dna seidob fo
seihpargopot ,erised fo seigolopot ,stnemom lla ,raeppasid sevil fo
sevaehs ,sraeppasid taht yalpsid cinagro ni selor gniyalp-xes

strap dna stnemhcatta fo tesolc drawyaw ym ni si srotcev dna sedon fo
selbat llams ruoY

refinneJ-uluJ em gninrut - strap dna stnemhcatta fo tesolc ym otni spees

tsaerb ruoY

sey sey sey sey sey::secruos rewen ot tniop nettirw retteb seulav fo esu
eht ylerus ,eert eht fo edis rehto eht fo tsdim eht ni ro dnoyeb eb tsum
taht uluj raed gnihtemos s'ereht ,neercs eht gnigrembus seulav ralacs fo
egnar a:esle gnihton dna refinnej tseraed refinnej raed oohoob seitnap ym
ni gnitirw ma i nehw tew yrev yrev eb lliw i won ,uluj raed ,tros taht fo
gnihtemos ro seireuq gnoma snoitairts ro senil fo gnitsil a ro ?erus eb ot
,secruos eseht fo yreuq ro noitseuq a syawla s'ereht:ssel ron erom rehtien
dna ecno desu gnihtemos ton fi ,sevlesruo tuoba yas i dluohs tahw ro ,txet
fo ydob eht ,uluj tseraed ,ydob eht tuohguorht ro ssorca gnilwarc slatineg

dna sevitineg ,sevitcejda dna snuon ,eseht sa erutalctnemom ro tnemom a
hcus eb ereht dluohs

refinnej tseraed ton yeht era ,seitnap gniporg era sdnah dna dnilb
gnilevart era ew ,no rehtruf dna tib tsethgils a tsuj tib tsethgils eht
tsuj ro ,okukin tseraed ,seitnap tsettew ym htiw dne eht yas i erehw siht
si ygde ym ni si sey sey sey sey sey erup ruoY

!ssel ron erom rehtien dna ecno desu gnihtemos ton fi ,sevlesruo tuoba yas
i dluohs tahw ro ,txet fo ydob eht ,uluj tseraed ,ydob eht tuohguorht ro
ssorca gnilwarc slatineg dna sevitineg ,sevitcejda dna snuon ,eseht sa
erutalctnemom ro tnemom a hcus eb ereht dluohs gniytrap eht-fo-uluj sey
sey sey sey sey erup ruoveD

crux

Julu's really something! Give up!
Yo! Dweeb! Whatever!
Cyberpunk or skatepunk?
You're out of your mind! Get lost!
A put-down, put out!
Put up with it on the spot!
Get real, blow up!
I can't get through to you - get it through your head?
Do you two get along? The deal goes sour.
Mind games - It got out of hand!
Chill! Get up!
Let's get down - nail someone!
I got to the bottom of it, twisted mind.
He gives me the creeps - spare me!
I got the jump on him - sleazebag!
We got down to business, scumbag.
Get off my case, screw lose.
Don't give me your lip, you're chicken.
We gave him the slip - you're out of your skull.
Julu's not herself recently - what's gotten into her?
Julu's really messed up.
He's caught between a rock and a hard place.
I didn't give it a second thought, boy-toy.
I want to get my hands on him! Gay, queer!
Techie - he's a total freak, he's packing a gun!
He gets hot under the collar, he's a real hothead!
Stop gawking! I'm spaced out.
I really lost it, bar-hopping; I'm really wasted.
Naked? Call an ambulance!

1,2,3 sequences

1, universal slaughterhouse of the scrawl

death is accompanied by the annihilation of memory, the annihilation of death. the political economy of death: I will Julu Twine to you; I will Nikuko Dojoji to you. Nikuko Dojoji passes beneath the sign of Alan, Alan Dojoji, another quality of identification that disappears. The beginning of cache-drawing in Second Life, the opening of the maw of the true world, virtual real, is gray mass, gray goo, outlines devoid of color. What is discernible is the growing, cawing, of memory always already at work signifying what is to come: proper names for these puppets or extensions, these flesh-works redolent of the human. Inscribe Julu Twine, and that is hir beginning and ending; hir cunt is dry fold in protocol codework dead-space; hir skin tears at the seams. Look closely and frisson disappears into ridging, swollen rips in the fabric of visual presence. Look closer and real slaughter begins.

2, invasions

torso-moss destruction of a great nation.
an environment for all ages and ideologies.
a platform for espousal of new ideas.
a compilation of redolent primitivism.
one-sided imaginary of dream-world imagery.
armies of the non-economic.
ruptured slaughterhouse of sea and island.
political economic of bandwidth bandits.

These will stop. These will come to an end, these experiments in space, time, movement, bandwidth, interaction, perception, virtuality. These will absolutely stop. These will absolutely come to an end.

From the concrete, steel, and brick building of the Virtual Environments Laboratory to the invisible, transparent, physical, translucent, and opaque manifolds of the virtual reality of Second Life - this is a complex domain of phenomenological experimentation that continues to expand and surprise.

3, Julu Twine sky-writer

Julu emits particle torso smoke, black smoker as undersea, seabottom, airless; hir movements sky-write fluidly and beautifully for everyone to see. I can demonstrate live in Second Life; let me know when you might be present - fully opened, fully closed

Julu Twine was tuned and retuned; the particle spew was moved from abdomen to chest - the bvh files had more movement in that region than in the pelvis, which was near the root node, and therefore fairly quiescent. Once the move was made, the invisible generator attachment was slid back into the area of the womb, since birth occurs in the tuning and retuning. What then? For the most part, a simulacrum or masquerade of a womb or pelvis or abdomen node. Symptoms develop: on occasion the source of torso generation moves from womb to a position outside the body of Julu Twine; it's following the chest, not the womb, and therefore a displacement occurs. Now with spawn - which is just that, spawn from loins as displacement from chest - it's possible to see Julu Twine in mid-air with full movement, and Julu Twine confined in an enclosed watery depression between building and earth. In the confinement, there is shuddering; in the shuddering, there is masquerade and continuous torso production which appears to emerge freely from the space, a signal or at the very least, a sign. But this emergence, this torso, itself is a fantasm; it's nothing more than a texture, a detailed square patch which appears, from certain angles, to possess weight, dimension, volume. So this is one fantasm among many, but a fantasm which goes nowhere; it can't be grasped in Second Life and such couldn't be grasped anywhere. So the shuddering, this apparent simulacrum of sex, this byproduct of confinement according to the codes and protocols of Second Life, produces a signal and a frisson among non-existent bodies, perhaps among viewers, perhaps a thrill or shudder, again, at the birth of a symptom. It's this symptom, this excess of desire in confinement and plein air, that disturbs, is read, goes nowhere - and goes nowhere because of its autonomy, autonomic nervousness, autonomic neurosis, railroad kidney and railroad spine and the like. It's what appears to be a chance result of programming; it's in reality the uneasy confluence of programming and interoperability, and collisions among programs. I take full responsibility, at the same time releasing Julu Twine to hir own amazing ends. Now I dream Julu Twine, I no longer know my own sex, but I own to no other and know no other, nor an other; it's all uncomfortable and dis/eased masquerade, something tawdry that I simultan- eously turn towards and away from, something in my character, a virus or parasite, a parasite of alterity, dreams of others, incandescent.

Liminal, slow

There are liminal moments when real and virtual intersect in a contrary and wayward matter, when Second Life, or any other program, isn't quite loaded, is only half present. Like the older work of jodi.org, the user's attention turns half towards immersion, and half towards anomaly - simultaneous tacit knowledge and paradox. Usually these moments are quick; sometimes they are slow, even permanent. There are also liminal spaces, which might be defined as equivalent, but there are also liminal spaces at game's edge, whether formed by island or height. Again, anomaly occurs; everything is problematic.

As I type this, I look out the window; there are light cumulus clouds in the dusk sky, reminiscent of Second Life dusk - but only if the Quality and Performance slider is set high; otherwise, the sky is blank, tawdry, unreal in any life. Here is yet another limit, and there are similar limits built into the software itself - details aren't all that fine, but as usual with avatars and landscapes, blank out into pixel-mania, no matter what the bandwidth. (And dreams? How are these configured; if one spends hours in Second Life, what happens then, if anything?)

(SPACE)
PLEASE, I BEG YOU.
(SPACE)
THIS TEXT IS CREATED BY JULU TWINE, ALAN DOJOJI, ALAN SONDHEIM. WE BEG YOU, IMPLORE YOU, TO TAKE THIS TEXT - ONE WAY OR ANOTHER - PRESERVE IT OFFLINE.. INSCRIBE IT IN METAL, PHOTOGRAPH IT (SILVER FILM ONLY), TURN IT WITH OAK AND LATHE; PAINT IT WITH ARCHIVAL PAINTS ON ARCHIVAL CANVAS. THE BEST IS BRONZE: CARVED IN BRONZE, IT MIGHT SURVIVE.
(SPACE)
OTHERWISE, IT IS LOST, THIS ONE REMNANT OF OUR WRITING; OUR NAMES - AND LET US NOT FORGET NIKUKO, JENNIFER, TRAVIS, AND CLARA - ARE LOST AS WELL.
PRESERVE MY NAMES, I BEG YOU. LET SOMETHING REMAIN.
(SPACE)

answering no one's critique +

To the criticism that my approach to Second Life is naive, apolitical ahistorical, and so forth: let me say this in my defense - that if one desires to study the phenomenology of any grouping of organisms, before * the overt socio-cultural issues are analyzed, it's necessary to understand the basics of their way of living, their space-time comprehension of whatever might pass for the real. To understand primates, for example, one might study their groupings (nations), customs, and conflicts in relation to strained resources - but one might study, first, their mode of being in the world, of which groupings, customs, and conflicts are at best only a developing part. ** The culture, the intrinsic and extrinsic political economy of Second Life, *** or any virtual world, are critical, but first comes the phenomenology of being-virtual in relation to the structural basics of that world. I realize I'm begging the question, that one can and does argue for political economy and culture, for that matter, all the way down - I've done that repeatedly myself. **** But the phenomenology and reach of virtuality is far greater and deeper than these institutions, ***** although entangled and inhering within and without them; I want to look at what's possible, what a user might extend or expand towards, should s/he or he inhabit the psychological, physical, and phenomenological limits of a space. ****** Physiology, neurophysiology, psychogeography, topography, sexuality, for examples - abjection, debris, edge phenomena, server phenomena in relation to all of these. Later, although simultaneous, construction, configuration, intrinsic and extrinsic economies, corporate and political affiliations and hacking, community and communality, interfacing with other worlds including the physical. ******* It's the latter, institutionalization, deterritorialization, and so forth, that constitutes most of the analyses I've read ******** - issues of the rational or at least psychoanalytical and normative subject, ********* however defined. Problematizing these in relation to delirium, frisson, dirt, flight, coherency, primary identifications and narcissisms if such exist - these are areas I scuttle about, beneath the surface of the _thing._ As example, _I, Avatar_'s description of sexuality in terms of groups, wars, dialogs, narrative, but not in terms of arousal, ejaculation, sexual triggers, uneasy dreams, worlds falling apart. I know, here, I'm not expressing myself clearly (I'm writing under severe depression and a kind of mental chaos), ********** but the distinction's there and more than lip-service is needed in relation to what humans are doing to themselves on a fundamental level within the concretization of fantasm, the uncanny, the untoward. *********** My site attempts ************ experiencing and thinking through these things by circumscribing what's recognizable, navigable, accountable, and unaccountable, in both the physical world and these fully-inscribed worlds (protocols and code all the way down *************) that surface and run (are refreshed, refresh-rate **************) in the midst of potential muck that may, for the participant, *************** problematize that very inscription (purity, in other words, towards impurity, acceptance towards stigma, clarity towards loss). (Don't worry, no one can do everything; the problem of course is if what's done bypasses or occludes inherent and necessary connections to what isn't. ****************)

+ small caps = false humility!
* as if there were a sequence here!
** "only"? begging the question!
*** there's a difference?!
**** irrelevant call to what history?!
***** absurd! this sort of qualification/quantification is nonsense!
****** again, a false mathesis, false geometrics here!
******* what is this "later"? why these levels, sequences, excuses?!
******** specious and suspicious lack of references!
********* seriously implying a relationship here?!
********** first, making excuses! second, bad analysis of _I, Avatar_!
*********** bad analysis - how and why are these things "concretized"?!
************ false humility, the worse sort of rhetorical trope!
************* here we go again with false geometrical analogy!
************** absurd extension based on similar roots!
*************** why? another red herring!
**************** another excuse! footnotes, self-condemnation!

Julu's home enTwined

julu emits particle torso smoke, black smoker as undersea, seabottom,
depth analysis of deep-sea black smoker interiors, airless response.

julu lives and works on a small square or spit of land attached to
nothing.

land sucks up everything, land is it.
water sucks up the land. the sea is indefinite, nothing lives there,
nothing visible, not now. perhaps later you might find someone, something,
take your time.

it's all confusing. one misstep, and s/he's lost hir bearings. the flat
sun rises and sets, glaring, subdued. weather might come later.
or a cool breeze.
the sun and moon cast shadows. there must be waxing or waning moons,
eclipses, crescents. i don't remember any of them.
julu only knows full and emptied sky, no thunderstorms, lightning.
not yet, nothing programmed by lindenlabs.

things might come later.
julu waits for the rain.

julu, pierced

was a bit difficult to set this up and julu had to wear hir flight
bracelet but we (Julu and I) managed to take these aerials from
around 650 meters up - it might not seem that high, but with the
use of false perspective we might as well have run up the kilometers.

over and over again, imagining this abject site until i'm exhausted,
julu's exhausted, nikuko's exhausted. this can't go on much farther,
can it. i can jam the site until everything halts, i lose my account,
julu disappears forever. i can slow up things uselessly - you'd have
to return two weeks from now to see any changes. at night my dreams
are distorted, julu doesn't have any, but she's in them. s/he walks
in fevers like the night.

daggers, that's what's shooting out. nikuko, blind, the rest of us.

i keep reading about second life, it's something else, not mine; i'm
waiting for the axe to fall, alan supine, imagine.

archetype starwoman lightwoman Julu lights up the sky, light furiously cascades around her, back home in Brooklyn, it's dark, lights off, it's as if the bombs are falling everywhere, as if we're huddled in the dark, net down, power off, nothing but these memories, they'll disappear soon. once one point I thought memories the most obdurate matter of all, my mother, for example, and hir world, inconceivably rich, the depth of any other, then that, crashing down with hir somewhat sudden death, now s/he resides in objects and objects dispersed, the skein is broken, so quickly and so corroded.

my own world's time and its historiography, I can't recognize myself, dear Julu. with starwoman lightwoman perhaps something remains, sears itself, at least in my mind, there was _that_ image and _that starwoman,_ and my mother's voice and for how long. the blacker my depression, unmeasured darkworld, the more light separates, bubbles forth, the more the froth of the bubbles, the more memory of childhood, a day, for example, on a tricycle on a sidewalk, myself rocking back and forth, the green of trees, white of cement, black of tricycle.

starwoman lightwoman takes me somewhere else dear God I do not want to see myself hear myself, dear God I do not want to live like this forever, not even for a year month a week minute second, atom clock hum stopped in disbelief at the first and present onslaught of an energized particle from distant Julu star, invisible to Julu, out of Julu world and stopping Julu breath as well

I, Julu, Hebrides

I will not live to see the sucking of the maw destroying local cosmos in someone's grasping craw.

Julu dies idea-wise fucking law deploying yokals' cosmos dumbed unwon and basking flaw.

Nikuko flies hir sucking jaw spoiling hokum cosmos summed and flown through untasked haw.

Alan lies hir chucking paw boiling cum's cosmos bummed, honed, and moaned, stewed unmasked gnaw.

Jennifer sighs burrs, mucking daw soiling, hummed cosmos stoned and groaned, rude sun tasked and yaw.

Menni surmise myrrhs, Jucking maw moiling, mummed cosmos moaned, manned, moaned, mewed mun masked, manned, maw.

GLORY

glory spews glory-wood baby; bleared 4-dim glory smeared across time : I cd not have done this work without the aid abet and glory of the American Emyre : glory pants inside glory pants out : time zone change: EST: pants inside-out < glacial intrusion: wet panties of Jennifer Glory, glorious [caliber of yr bullet [traceroute trace :skins fly thru the air there, cd fly thru it, Julu says, cum up for air, Julu is Oedipus mad, Julu-Carthaginian < so Nikuko's ground-level black smoker in the fucked-up world of Migraine-Toulouse, s/he sings If you ever cum this way again / watch out women watch out men / a plant planted leaves seeds and roots / smokers dye w/ rotted fruits > friends and Carthaginians give me yr skins & sing about the glory of better daze : time zone change: EST: 3 a.m. when it's the dark nite of the soul ::there's no glory in what i do, there's no glory in me or you, there's no glory in my bloody art, there's no glory on my bloody part, shadows everywhere for me and you, shadows everywhere is what Julu do, shadows skyward in a flock, shadows skyward hard as rock, there's no glory hole whole, there's no body whole, there's nobody's hole, there's no glorymachine ::

Your the ecstatis mary comes crimpled all skinned rezzed generous mary, what is 3 d 2 b? is in-me my where

ecstatis mary comes crimpled all skinned rezzed generous mary, what is 3 d 2 b?

Your impossible connects my ecstatis mary comes crimpled all skinned rezzed generous mary, what is 3 d 2 b? with needle park

yr dealing with fuck-driven ecstatic glory cum-crumpled Alan Skin, says Jennifer Glory, what is 2 b dun? ecstatic glory cum-crumpled Alan Skin, says Jennifer Glory, what is 2 b dun? ecstatis mary comes crimpled all skinned rezzed generous mary, what is 3 d 2 b? ecstatis mary comes crimpled all skinned rezzed generous mary, what is 3 d 2 b?

sex-playing roles in organic display that disappears, sheaves of nodes and vectors is in my wayward closet of attachments and parts

Your small tables seeps into my closet of attachments and parts - turning me Julu-Jennifer

Your breast

should there be such a moment or momentclature as these, nouns and adjectives, genitives and genitals crawling across or throughout the body, dearest julu, the body of text, or what should i say about ourselves, if not something used once and neither more nor less:there's always a question or query of these sources, to be sure? or a listing of lines or striations among queries or something of that sort, dear julu, now i will be very very wet when i am writing in my panties boohoo dear jennifer dearest jennifer and nothing else:a range of scalar values submerging the screen, there's something dear julu that must be beyond or in the midst of the other side of the tree, surely the use of values better written point to newer sources::yes yes yes yes yes

Your pure yes yes yes yes yes is in my edgy is this where i say the end with my wettest panties, dearest nikuko, or just the slightest bit just a slightest bit and further on, we are traveling blind and hands are groping panties, are they not dearest jennifer

Devour pure yes yes yes yes yes julu-of-the partying should there be such a moment or momentclature as these, nouns and adjectives, genitives and genitals crawling across or throughout the body, dearest julu, the body of text, or what should i say about ourselves, if not something used once and neither more nor less!

GLORY SPEWS GLORY-WOOD BABY
MEAT ME THERE

for hir we are dy9ing and the calling-forth

for hir, we are dy9ing

for hir, we are dy9ing, ju# k: kill all unconnected #g gladly, let me have your breast, let me drink from # o: options # and endings we are waifs, we are wayward,, we are mi# r: rering all # shit nor drink, wears us like a glove, # s: shell ## u: user list # we think hir thoughts only# w: output user to file #ly, taste hir sweet tongue ah ah ah ah ah we are, niu# q: quit #

############################

nikuko, our mouths open for hir, oh that s/he would dying of thirst in desiccation, oh s/he must be satisifed, must s/he not! where and when we suffer, suckle me, julu, let me bleed open for you and there, drink my blood, my bitter tears are openings for your speech, julu, we are contrary children, neither piss, nikuko, nor eat, we do nothing,

our mistress only, julu, suck hirsweet sweet flesh only, ah ah ah ah ah we are julu, ah ah ah ah ah

[Nikuko and Julu, both emanents of a single mistress/master; they're different but inhabited similarly; they are equally opened; mistress peers inside them; they're splayed for hir; they are lovers sharing equivalent bodies; they're four-dimensional beings whose interiors open to any viewer daring to come close enough; they are both worn like gloves; they participate on the surface in sado-masochisms; they have no will of their own; they have given up will; they never had it in the first place; they speak through me; they meld; their dreams, our desires ...]

the calling-forth

[ringing ...]
[Waiting for connection...]
[11;1Hif i could not write, i would be dead; it's necessary to signify my
life.
a life isn't worth living,,
 Nikuko, if it were dead or such beyond. you must wai
wait here with me, int
 this space residing with me.
[8Bwaiting if i could not write, julu, signifies nothing. i would write
your body,
your body imminent; i would write your body now, uncover it in one virtual
worl
world after another, skin emptied of all thought -
[Kemptied of all thought except for me, Julu, you within e
me as our mistress, whom
whomever, takes us on like a glove,
[14Cone after another, same think
thinking and no escape, same tune and no horizon
[36Cand no air, Nikuko, and no breathing, no br
breath, nothing but the hold our mistress
[7Chas upon us, julu, taking our
bodies one after another, wearing them visibile and invisible,
[42Cfucking our bodies, julu, sliced open
for hir, available to hir on every level, prim and primitive, hir body
, hir body prime fo
for receptioon
n, hir we
ait
[39Cours alone, niku
nikuko, our mouths open for hir, oh that s/he would
[24Cpiss on us, water us i t
n this desert, our mouths wide fo
for hir, we are dy9ing, julu,
[21Cdying of thirst in desiccat
desiccation, oh s/he must be satisfied, must s/he not! where and when we
suffer,
[30Cnikuko, hardly suffering gladly, let me have your
[9;1Hbreast, let me drink from it,

[18;1Hsuckle me, julu, let me bleed open for you and there, drink my
blood, my bitter
[18;1Htears are openings for your speech,
[30Cour sadness, beginn
nings and ed
ndings we are waifs,
[36Cjulu, we are contrary children,
[8Bwe are wayward,, we are misery themselves, we neither shit or d
nor drink,
neither pis
piss, nikuko, nor eat, we do nothing,
[18;1Hour ms
istress
[70Cwears us
[9;1Hlike a glove,
[9;1Hwe think hir thoughts only, move hir arms and legs u
only, taste hir sweet tongue
[13Conly, julu, suck hir sw
irsweet sweet flesh only, ah ah ah ah ah
[8Bah ah ah ah ah we are, niuko
kuko,
[40Cwe are
[Jjulu, ah ah ah ah ah
[32Cah ah ah ah ah

[Waiting for connection...]
if i could not write, i would be dead; it's necessary to signify my life.
[8Ba life isn't worth living,,
Nikuko, if it were dead or such beyond. you must wai
wait here with me, int
this space residing with me.
waiting if i could not write, julu, signifies nothing. i would write your
body,
your body imminent; i would write your body now, uncover it in one virtual
worl

world after another, skin emptied of all thought -
[Jemptied of all thought except for me, Julu, you within e
me as our mistress, whom

whomever, takes us on like a glove,
[50Cone after another, same think
thinking and no escape, same tune and no horizon
[13Dand no air, Nikuko, and no breathing, no br
breath, nothing but the hold our mistress
[49Chas upon us, julu, taking our
bodies one after another, wearing them visibile and invisible,
[21Dfucking our bodies, julu, sliced open
for hir, available to hir on every level, prim and primitive, hir body

, hir body prime fo
for receptioon
n, hir we
ait
[63Cours alone, niku

nikuko, our mouths open for hir, oh that s/he would
[27Dpiss on us, water us i t
n this desert, our mouths wide fo
for hir, we are dy9ing, julu,
[51Cdying of thirst in desiccati
desiccation, oh s/he must be satisfied, must s/he not! where and when we suffer,
[49Dnikuko, hardly suffering gladly, let me have your
[18;1Hbreast, let me drink from it,
[9;1Hsuckle me, julu, let me bleed open for you and there, drink my blood, my bitter
[9;1Htears are openings for your speech,
[6Dour sadness, beginn
nings and ed
ndings we are waifs,
[36Cjulu, we are contrary children,
[9Bwe are wayward,, we are misery themselves, we neither shit or d
nor drink,
[68Cneither pis
piss, nikuko, nor eat, we do nothing,
[9;1Hour ms
istress
[57Cwears us
[18;1Hlike a glove,
[18;1Hwe think hir thoughts only, move hir arms and legs u
only, taste hir sweet tongue
[13Conly, julu, suck hir sw
irsweet sweet flesh only, ah ah ah ah ah
[9Bah ah ah ah ah we are, niuko
kuko,
[72Cwe are
[Kjulu, ah ah ah ah ah
[11Cah ah ah ah ah

[Nikuko and Julu, both emanents of a single mistress/master; they're different but inhabited similarly; they are equally opened; mistress peers inside them; they're splayed for hir; they are lovers sharing equivalent bodies; they're four-dimensional beings whose interiors open to any viewer daring to come close enough; they are both worn like gloves; they participate on the surface in sado-masochisms; they have no will of their own; they have given up will; they never had it in the first place; they speak through me; they meld; their desires, our dreams ...]

Confusion

The exhibition arena hall and skysphere are clumped, colluded, coagulated, confused, contorted, convoluted, complicated, occluded, obscured, obfuscated, and obstructed - to such an extent that editing at this point becomes almost impossible; an editor, myself through Julu or Nikuko (Alan Dojoji), literally can't see ahead, with or without mouselook, sufficiently to isolate and link individual prims. Everything is spewing against or towards everything else and the high-speed movement (rotatory, linear, in combination) of objects results in jumps from position to position; they remain ungraspable. It's also increasingly unclear as to what constitutes an object in the first place; particle spews are everywhere, as are alien permissions that refuse to be modified.

There are also slow-ups as a result of increasing bandwidth; Second Life - in other words my access to the representation of the virtual world - almost grinds to a halt at times. Think of over 2000 particles each carrying a video texture and moving at high-speed from sources that are also moving at high speed, among say, 300 three-dimensional and partially transparent prims (also moving, etc.), and you get the idea. So there is a shift in attention, from proper construction or deconstruction to the maintenance, management, and configuration of a miasma which can barely be grasped in whole or in part.

I think of this as a form of information implosion where everything gets out of hand, or a war or sex zone where it's impossible to walk or think, or Pliny's uncle's death (and other devastation) when Vesuvius blew: What does one do in such a situation? How does one do it? One false step or click and you're underwater or in the skysphere (which is a bit quieter than the thirteen channels of sound competing for your attention on the ground floor - not to mention video, if you have that turned on as well), finding or fighting your way back and to what? - More of the same, an incandescent Las Vegas teetering on the brink of the apocalyptic with no way out, and possibly no way in for that matter. Because the entrance itself shimmers, dances, and roars, and it's easier to fly through the melange than to attempt walking or running in - neither may be possible from time to time. Then consider this, and what do you do or see when you get there? Some things, some prims, moving out of the way, vanishing or almost vanishing - it depends on size and location. And for that matter, you might not be able to recognize the vanishing at all - there are always things coming in to take their place, coming at you, furiously fleeing you, or so it seems. The wonder for me, other than the beauty in coagulation, decay and concentration, is that all of this occurs within a small and somewhat stabilized space, a column in a sense, ascending from ocean through deconstructed architecture to skysphere - neither above the skysphere nor below the ocean nor beneath the ground - anyway - all of this occurs in a relatively contained space, and yet seems everywhere, everywhen, a concussion of simultaneities which appear self-defining, and simultaneously topologically/topographically open ad closed, a machine extending from micro- to macro-cosm, and yet doing nothing but high-speed processing and representation of scripts that appear to be running amuck, but are in fact quite logical from the interior, if in fact there is an interior, which is also, in the midst of all this craziness, up and down for grabs.

I Own my World

From: Second Life
To: Alan Dojoji <sondheim@panix.com>
Subject: Second Life - the object 'Second Life' has sent you a message

The object 'Second Life' has sent you a message from Second Life:
Your object 'Object' has been returned to your inventory lost and found folder from parcel 'Odyssey_ExhibitA_Gallery_zone1' at Odyssey 26, 4.
= Second Life is owned by Julu Twine
= http://slurl.com/secondlife//0/0/0

Entering

To get into The Accidental Artist catastrophe site, it's best to fly in. At one point years ago, it was possible to access the ground floor by taking the front stairs; after these began their slow precession, it seemed possible at times to wait, then climb when they were properly positioned. Now, everything's different; the stairs are treacherous and you might find yourself beneath the ground, drowning without a clue, shapes falling, rotating, and shuddering around you, choke choke. Best as I said to fly in. At another point months ago, that was easier to do, flying ahead across the threshold, entering the space, it's 'turned to stone' perhaps or deconstructed, or less treacherous, you could always be assured of air. At yet another point weeks ago, better to fly above, how high is that, above the space, the walls, the particles, the objects, the translucencies, the part-objects, fly above I say, then descend, slowly and carefully and to be sure unlosing oneself or winning oneself back, unfacing oneself, descend certainly and unsurely, through an artificial air that sounds like you're there, somewhere to be sure, the air is cold, warm yourself, the air is cold. Then to the colder light and buffeting, you might, you will, lose your footing, and I, myself, I can no longer edit objects which escape, love to disappear, were told to disappear, we're happy, we're not threatened, we're really happy, so much light and color! so much sound. I make myself lose myself, Julu said, and I lose you too.

Prick

It was difficult to attach the prick.
The object wouldn't adjust to hir proper position.
The object crept up the legs creeping down.
The object continued to flux.
The texture spewed across the object.
The texture spread everywhere.
The object rotated too fast or too slow.
The object glowed too much are disappeared into shadow.
The texture was too grayed out or too brilliant.
The prick was slanted in an awkward direction.
The tip of the prick was difficult to view.
The prick was misaligned with the body.
Two or more pricks would appear at the same time.
Less than one prick appeared in rotation.
The object was too round or not round enough.
The object appeared to detach itself.
The object was invisible and embedded.
Aligning the prick separated the object from Julu.
The prick seemed a separate and independent object.
The prick seemed too short or too long.
The texture was misaligned on the object.
The prick appeared too hard or too soft.
The object rotated with misaligned axes of rotation.
The object yawed during rotation.
The prick was invisible or far too visible.
The prick wasn't sufficiently succulent.
The prick disappeared into a blood-red matrix.
The sphere was deformed too radically.
The hole of the sphere was misaligned with the body.
The hole of the sphere was insufficiently vaginal.
The interior of the hole was too large or too small.
The texture of the hole was too ornamental.
The texture of the hole was unreadable.
There were too many pricks in the hole texture.
The hole wasn't succulent enough.
The hole was too geometrical.
The object was too spherically regular.
The object emerged on the other side of the body.
The object almost disappeared into the body.
The prick was too small or too large.
The fit was too loose or too tight.
Nobody appreciated the prick like Julu Twine.
The prick was hir prick and belonged to hir.
Julu Twine made it hir own.
This was the second prick of Julu Twine.
The first prick of Julu Twine went out of world.
The first prick was not returned.

barb the dart, bore, burn, discolor, defuge, excite, girdle pain, gore, hurt the feelings, impale, inflict pain, itch, kill by inches, martyr, obscure, pang, poke, prolong the agony, rankle, ride herd on, rowel, scum, seal, skewer, slit, speckle, spike, spurt, tattoo mark, terminate, thrill, tingle tangle, tip, transfix, transpierce, trepan, watermark, whip, wound, wrangle

skysphere transformation

in the skysphere godsphere,
i am there now, come see, while i,
i breathe nothing; sightless am i, and unhearing.
i am caught there, cauterized, nothing beneath
the torso, neither to the left nor right am i,
neither above or below, before or behind.
i am only what you see, and how or what you see,
is how i am.

The say which is the thing of Alan that is Julu and Nikuko

Julu and Alan and Nikuko and landscape no comment
Julu and Nikuko together
Julu and Alan together
Landscapes after the fashion
Nikuko and Alan together in the landscape
Julu in the landscape
Julu and Nikuko in the featureless landscape no comment
no comment, I've abjured my responsibility. that is to say -
to say what, countered Julu? to say that you talk too much, let pictures do the talking.
to counter this Nikuko insisted that responsibility lay in continuing to provide, provide what? to provide an edge that you lie against or on, your body almost ready to fall, teetering on the brink beneath which there are only rocks, or water, or water and rocks at the base of the cliff.
Nikuko insisted that this is about the cliff, there's no rest, no respite, nothing but the yaw of the cliff as the point of view changes
in translation.
the point of view in the featureless landscape, no comment.
no comment in julu or nikuko, they are given nothing to say.

they must be given something to say.
someone must give them something to say.
someone who does not appear in the featureless landscape, no comment.
someone Alan who tenders them, they are spies on the edge of a nervous breakdown.

they are spies.
Alan lets them loose, they report back, or, no comment, Alan reports back, their reaction, their place and presence, their signifier, their name and sign and if lucky, their universal identification number, good for all encounters.
Alan who owns the virtual world, no comment, Alan has no identification.
Julu and Nikuko carry their identification across the featureless landscape, carry it in world.
Alan may give them something to say and they are not pleased or unpleased to say it, they are only of the saying of it, they are the saying of it.
Across the featureless landscape, Alan and Julu and Nikuko, no comment.

Her Master

Julu is uncomfortable with these and I know, in my heart of hearts, I should be as well. For I would not want to change places with her for the world. I would not want to be so humble or dependent. It's true we're all dependent, but surely there are limits? And this is past my limit, outside, so to speak, of my "comfort zone." Yet s/he must be used to these things; s/he was born with them and most likely will die with them. What am I to do, but continue on? What am I to do?

Bvh file behavior collision traced in 'mid-air'

It's four ai/em in the morning, past the dark night of the soul; I am ashamed to read fiction, there's so little time left; my neck is in pain, my shoulders, those regions beneath the upper jaw, my left leg and foot as usual. The greater the dusk, the greater the rush of voices and ignorance on my part, not theirs. I work on useless problems - Second Life instead of the First for example, or this artificial physics instead of the real, concrete world we've been thrown into, our first lack of choice as death of course is our last.

In this Second Life I can at least comprehend since I'm a surgeon here. In all this world the cut's the thing, dreams following suit. So I thought myself a myth, that of colliding behaviors, Julu for example doing neither one thing nor another, but then it seemed... it seemed as if it was just that, another myth. So I put it to the test and within Second Life, as within the First, of which the Second is but a part or excuse or poor actor - within Second Life, as I was saying, a double bind produces - not the tension of stasis or sudden and catastrophic collapse to one or another mode of behaving, being, because in Second Life, _behaving is being_ - but a confusion of behaviors, an army of nodes gone amuck, deep distortion of figuration here as nothing is figured out. A fugue state's inverted, the body twists and turns - neither organized nor disorganized, neither one nor the other, that is to say perhaps the Sheffer stroke - Neither A nor B - and that is to say the appearance of the dual - both A and B, and yes, the order's non-symmetrical as (A)(B) does not equal (B)(A). Isn't this some sort of breakdown, one without the other, not the Sheffer, as fossils, remnants, are manifest, and then perhaps the dual? This is a mess, it's the mess at work, since Sheffer and dual break down here - what emerges isn't synergetic either - just something untoward, unpredictable, bordering, but not quite, on the chaotic. What does this mean except that if extrapolated to the real we'd have the same type of complexity suddenly appearing as in Wolfram's automata - that might be a bit close to the real then, the Second melding into the First, as the Second, noted above, is already within the First, if not the First enveloping the Second. It's confusing, deeply so, inherently so, and the evidence is clear in the images below, the clarity of A, the roughness of B perhaps and the contamination of each by the other, the irruption of confusion in the trails left behind.

I can't think clearly beyond this, only to note that the ability to think itself will draw to a close, that soon there will be a dawn and I will be blind and thoughtless, and that will be the end of it, confusion as well, and I will not be present for that end or the pretense of purity which might, for some, follow it, follow suit.

teeter

the big clock struck the hour of doom
the small clock struck the hour of gloom
all of us heard the distant boom
as the boom was lowered and the room
shrank plank to plank and the flume
burst in the gloom of a womb
and doom as flooding made a tomb
from the room spurting a plume
of smoke choked and yoked to a fume
from the thunder's womb, va voom, va voom,
va voom, va voom, va voom, va voom.

Damned

When dark and drowned in fountain's red despair
I all alone construct my cast-off state,
I fly in Second Life to my unholy lair
And there rebuilt the world I love to hate -
My home! Absolved, I fly a solid sea,
Search nudes and textures, such frivolity! -

But for good purpose - a place to disappear -
And then to live and die in that good night
One can't walk gentle in; now avatars appear,
Caress and bend their prims in dawn's bleak light.
Please do not run from me; do not fear my eyes
Which glow; they only mirror skies
That split me open, spread me; I turn crust -
Caress my sheaves, fulfill my ruined lust.

Amazing Grounded Universes and Other Phenomena

Some skysphere spaces are interspersed among the objects in the Odyssey exhibition space. These spaces revolve slowly, are textured, can trap avatars attempting to negotiate them; they carry a mute symbolic which goes nowhere, as if it came from nowhere, instead of coming from already surfaced textures. But they're relatively enormous, part of the sky; you can hardly see Julu Twine living and moving among one of them. Good for Julu!

Julu: "These are so cool! In Second Life, where I am and you are too at times there for me, the Unwieldy doesn't exist! Something twenty stories high moves as quickly as a glove; a building behaves like a ball, a tree like a pebble or stone or plate; a tree like a picture, a picture of a tree. Everything runs on equal power here; no one gets sick, everyone will die, disappear. But for now on the hedge or ledge of things - take a look! - miracles occur in utmost safety... "

The New World

Julu Twine on the Asus eee pc 701 exploring Second Life - very small jpgs to be sure. What is it you can see? That s/he can ride hir own universes in the center of the exhibition space, s/he can add and subtract objects within them, s/he's there for us to be sure - Yes! And s/he has become once again dual-sexed, creating hir way across these spaces dedicated to the new Swiss collider to be sure that may in a very short time destroy all of us, but not really - just as the collider brings new phenomena to the foreground, fundamental, basic, ground-breaking phenomena, so do these tiny universes foreground behaviors that rest uneasy on the ground the rest of us walk on; think of Julu Twine as Pioneer of the Virtual, s/he explores phenomena we can only dream of, bends protocols to hir Will, walks and experiences space-time invisible to the rest of us, perhaps someday s/he will write hir memoirs, they will be poor substitutions for the real thing, but as close as we can get, closer than we are now: Julu!

For our sakes! ...

urges

These images: articulation dots; Yamantaka; avatar construction plans, Poser speeds endlessly through the body - I love these feelings - images: articulation dots; Yamantaka; avatar construction plans; Poser... My avatars attempting to negotiate them; they carry a mute symbolic which is yours... as usual with avatars and landscapes, blank out into pixel-mania, no calls forth crawled, eating, core-dumping, in-you the where, as usual with avatars and landscapes, blank out into pixel-mania, no organs and grids crawled in here...

Are you properly compiling as usual with avatars and landscapes, blank out into pixel-mania, no ? For 1 day, I have been Julu... and it has taken you just 0.133 minutes turning on ... This Julu cries out of Titus Andronicus, will be forgotten. words lose tongues, speed endlessly through the body - I love these feelings, Julu cries out of Titus Andronicus, will be forgotten. words lose tongues... My sward, mobile and translucent - Julu says more organism! more organism! is yours... neither object nor clothing surface lovely Julu Twine! calls forth incandescent, eating, core-dumping.

Within , neither object nor clothing surface lovely Julu Twine! bark or stone, portend maternal fecundity, Julu Twine murmuring in - incandescent from the breasts - it's possible to see Julu Twine in mid-air with full - here, it's incandescent -

Are you properly compiling neither object nor clothing surface lovely Julu Twine? For 1 day, I've been dreaming Julu... and it has taken you just 0.133 minutes turning on...

This julu emits particle torso smoke, black smoker as undersea, seabottom, speeds endlessly through the body - I love these feelings. julu emits particle torso smoke, black smoker as undersea, seabottom - Would julu emit particle torso smoke, black smoker as undersea, seabottom, mind your wetware? My waiting if i could not write, julu, signifies nothing. i would write yours...

julu only knows full and emptied sky, no thunderstorms, lightning, calls forth the incandescent, eating, core-dumping put-you-in-me cocaine-you-know-me, julu only knows full and emptied sky, no thunderstorms, lightning, julu lives and works on a small square or spit of land attached to?

...incandescent is - suckle me, julu, let me bleed open for you and there, drink my blood, here, it's incandescent? Are you properly compiling julu only knows full and emptied sky, no thunderstorms, lightning?

Wait! julu only knows full and emptied sky, no thunderstorms, lightning. are gone forever! For 1 day, I have been where Julu ... and it has taken you just 0.133 minutes turning on...

GREAT UNIVERSES!

The Great Universes Stretch To The Sky!
Do Observe The Excitement Reigns!
Angels Would Be In Ecstasy To See Such Things!
Humans! Admire Your Creator!
Uncanny Events Sully The North East South West Skies!
North East West South Spells NEWS Of An Amazing Sort!
We Do Now Observe That God Observes Our Wondrous Creation!
God! Pray To Us Who Conquer Thee In Perfect Recompense!
Wherever We Look A Universe Begins!
Wherever We Do Not Look A Universe Comes to An End!
Of The Proofs There Are Many!
Of The Rites Of Visitation There Are Multitudes!
Worlds Of Fabulous Excitement!
Lands Of Fun and Ecstasy!
Organic Orgasm And Organs! Pinwheels Of Universal Stars!
Make A Visit You Will Never Regret!
A Visit Of A Lifetime! A Visit Of Unforgettable Memories!
Come to http://slurl.com/secondlife/Odyssey/48/12/22 !
Do Not Delay! Hesitate No Longer!
The Great Universes Stretch To The Sky!

Infinite

Goethe: "Whichever way you look at nature, it is the source of what is infinite." (Maxims and Reflections 1409, trans. Stopp.)

Julu: Yes, but of course in Second Life, there is no nature; things can only go so high.

Nikuko: Perhaps the idea is one of extrapolation, the asymptotic - one imagines going higher, and this is always the case. (Of course there is always dimensional collapse - the asymptotic grinding to a halt.)

Julu: Only to an extent - if nothing else the computer itself, client or server, carries its own limitations, and these are intrinsic, inherent, inherited.

Nikuko: This is responsible for what I consider the _compression_ of Second Life - the uncanny sensation that everything, no matter how distant, remains contained, closed in, closing in on itself, closing in on us, users and avatars and observers, for that matter.

Julu: And contained along the axis of equivalence or equivalent substance (shades of the analogic!), since it is all code, protocol, programming, program dynamics; it is all of a one or a two, of a type - one might say, following Kripke, of a _natural kind._

Nikuko: Yes, it is a digital substance or floating signifier - and a substance with malleable boundaries and internals, but one nonetheless having a limit or limits, compression. This is easier to see - witness - than in the physical world; inhabiting any virtual world, Second Life or other, always has a sense of poverty to it. Where one invests is ultimately in the language or culture - inscribing oneself in and out of it, so to speak/write/rewrite/presence onself.

Julu: The compression extends metaphorically to a lack of atmosphere - for that matter a lack of anything at all (shades of Nagarjuna!); what occurs, rides on any number of machines and conduits. As if the world were vacuum and emptied even of that.

Julu again: But it's this - I _sense_ it, this compression. In a way it seems unnatural, but it's all we have within what is, one way or another, a corroded, porous, and dynamic manifold. And it's suffocating.

Nikuko: It's suffocating and wounds; we live within a semantic manifold as well, one of permanent wounding.

Julu: And this is what I meant by _flattening,_ the flat world -

Nikuko: - which extends, seeps out, from the virtual, back into what one normally considers the real or Real (literally whatever, here); it is all compressed -

Julu: - abjection and defuge at the heart of it.

Nikuko: However one might want to define heart - whatever it is or seems to be, it's not infinite.

Julu: The idea of the 'true world' again, coming into play everywhere, inscribed or uninscribed.

Nikuko: I can't breath...

Julu: Nor I...

Julu Twine Pinup

Julu I want to have sex with you.
I want to have sex with you Julu Twine.
Stuttering, I dream of your taking me hard your skin all over me.
Shuddering, I dream of fucking you fucking me fucking you.

Shattering, I dream of scat and golden showers and audience and you.
Sputtering, I dream of my bondage not yours while you gag me.
Splattering, I dream of liquids pouring from your holes.
Spattering, I dream of your pulling the knot tighter and tighter.
Stumbling, I dream of masquerade and your cutting me open and wide.
Smothering, I dream of your choking me and your wet and heavy smell.
Shivering, I dream of your cum on me wiping me out and wiping me clean.
Spotting, I dream of greedily licking your shit from your asshole.
Scattering, I dream of swallowing your hot piss dribbling over me.
Shitting, I dream of your vomit and disdain and your disgust and fury.
I want to have sex with Julu Twine.
Julu I want to have sex with you.

Gearing of the universes

There's other stuff going on here; I don't remember all of it. Most of the large objects from duplications of the skysphere are revolving. Later the skysphere was revolving and the texture changed again; I didn't want my face in the sky anymore, I wanted Yamantaka's. But the image I think are fairly amazing now that the sphere and Alan Dojoji, who is Nikuko, are interacting. So things are going on in space that are fairly gravity-less, in some sort of freefall, although there's an object at the bottom of the skysphere which has been there for months and continues to remain in place. That seems to have weight. Weight of course is artificial but the skysphere appears as a sort of satellite. It's not, but it appears so. And if it were a satellite then an object in it wouldn't be free-floating, which it's not. Still, it's the only thing like that; the other objects float happily, as they do nearer the ground - as do the duplications and for that matter remnants of the skyspheres, all within the exhibition space proper, although extending upward and into the grounds in front of the building, some near the seawall but well above it. That's a feature of this particular virtual world, this floating - not to mention what appears to be a kind of perpetual, frictionless, energyless, motion of all the objects, some of which have been in a kind of hysteria, symptomology, for upwards of eleven weeks. Well, the motion isn't perpetual, of course; it's the result of client/server activity, protocols, code, programming, callups, and so forth. And that is fed from the electric grid, which draws on nuclear and coal energy for the most part - the motion, in other words, is the result of resource consumption. The energy is relatively miniscule, especially compared to the enormous amounts of energy it would take to move what seems to be close to a thirty-story apparatus, day and night, without monitoring or a caretaker. Of course I'm a caretaker of sorts, but I'm out of the space, have always been so. In any case, what you would see, should you choose to visit the space, is something even more marvelous than before, and you'd get to walk or fly around all of this without my presence, or anyone else's, no interference here -

Luminism

In the New World of Luminism, video paints and repaints the ocean; everywhere turmoil occurs and everywhere the sky is a deeper trouble.

Luminism of the cataract of Niagara and the eye, sublime mists, mists transformed into the commonplace of video texturing, virtual worlds!

For they are manifold and of a Spirit unbounded by code's compression, the weak evanescence of code, the languor of clouds and rainbows.

Suns, suns!

avatar, flowing, flow

sometimes Julu Twine's nudity is overwhelming.

what might be blood is the presence of the invisible.

what is hidden might be menstrual.
19th century Germany: male Jews had monthly discharges.

what's secreted is the object of desire, abject,
desultory.

from hir back is J.T. male or female? no one knows hir.
no one knows hir like hir handler. so difficult!

what is to be done?
these are simple images, sheave, red thud, pinwheel.

someone does someone's bidding. or not at all. who can
tell what the gods insist? the body is infinitely malleable,
almost; then a vessel is struck, tissue severed from tissue,
and days are needed to restore Julu Twine. here,
in our other world, under
a moon full with poisoned air, neither days nor years suffice;
things fall apart, everything falls and fails. memories are
slow to leave, of reds and browns and flowing, and those years

before when many suns whirled the hollow sky. now the ship
arrives, no one is prepared, and seeming worlds sink,
are drawn screaming, past agony; reds and browns flow
furiously, once again, and then no more.

Moving around gets harder and harder

On the ground floor you may teleport to the ground floor.
You may teleport from the ground floor to the skysphere or ocean inlet.
The ocean inlet is filled with prims with proximity scripts that have
desperately, it seems, tried too get out of the way.
You can hardly find your way there to the two spheres that send you
back to the surface.
On the surface you can barely find your way to the two spheres that
send you back to the ocean inlet.
Almost everything sends you somewhere else.
Almost everywhere sends you somewhere else.
Almost everywhere may send you almost everywhere, including where you
are, right now.
But to get there, you must enter, and enter everything.
And to enter is almost impossible, as flight is almost impossible;
remnants of skyspheres obstruct your every move.
You might try to fly around the slowly turning skyspheres.
You will most likely be caught in the slowly turning skyspheres.
If you have the proper gift, you can fly directly to the skyspheres.
Flying as such, you will move upwards along a chain of enormous
remnants of skyspheres, end on end, slowly wheeling in the sky.
You will find you cannot enter the skysphere from below or through the
sides; you must enter through the top, lowering yourself.
You will then stop flying, and walk around the cone penetrating the
floor, and you will walk with wonder.
You will walk with wonder at the solitude and beauty of the space.
You may touch any of the objects in the skysphere and you will be
transported back to the ground.
Or you may fly out of the top of the skysphere and move away from the
surface and look back; you will be amazed at the particle
streams and sky-writing that emanates from it.
Or you may fly out of the top of the skysphere, move slightly to the
sky, and allow yourself to fall beautifully down and into the
exhibition space, where you will right yourself in order to look about.
Within the exhibition space you will find everything and nothing to
see as your path is obstructed by objects and particles desperate to
get out of your way.
These objects that are desperate will end up at least in part within
the ocean inlet which you may have just visited.

There are songs and noise and as you move from one place to another within the ocean inlet or exhibition space the songs and noise will change.
There is video which streams across and within the streaming particles and you may turn the video on and off and the space of the exhibition utterly changes.
But you will barely see anything unless you separate your viewpoint from the viewpoint of the avatar or set your avatar to mouseview, in which case you are tied to the avatar bending
and moved by objects and streams blocking hir path, ascending to hir or descending upon hir.
You may find some of those objects sending your avatar down into the ocean inlet which you may or may not have already visited.
And you must beware of the trap by the stairs leading into the exhibition space, the trap which sends you into a part of the ocean inlet from which there is no return, none except for your teleporting back to your home space which you may or may not have set, and from your home space you may then teleport back into a safer area of the exhibition space.
There are so many traps like this, so many distorted and occluded views, so many shadows.
And so many shadows and peripheral darkness even in the middle of a dark dark day.
So you will walk around or through the shadows which depends on the nature of the shadows day or night, whatever time it is in the virtual world.
But it's all blooming, buzzing, confusion; it's all wildness that seems almost random; it's all bright lights and dimmed space; it's a small space you cannot lose; it's a small space that can lose you.
So you will be careful and your reward will be great, no, greater than that, and that with wonder.

Notes by an Space-artist

[rewritten from a previous text; it seems that avatar/body is transparent-space, inhering space, dynamic and malleable space -]

As space-artist, we are our space Jennifer-Julu-Nikuko-Travis-Alan and our space is us, both controlled by motion-capture behaviors using remapped sensors and moving at ultra-high-speeds among other spaces, landscapes, virtual worlds in the real, online, in one's mind.

But our space is unique, our space is tissue, our space transforms backwards and forwards at perceptually instantaneous speed between frames.
Our space is alien.

Jennifer: "our space has slimy space movement, wormlike shape-shifting, at warp high-speed perceptually conflated with itself, our space is speed-alien, malleable and originating tissue. as originating, our space is demiurge, producing and reproducing, originating worlds and gatherings of the true world."

Julu: "our space is disparaged body or bodies, our space is OTHERING, here and there moving asymptotically among fractal intrusions, our space prepares the appearance of twisted connected topologies, limit-sets of behaviors, topological counterexamples and distraught spaces piled upon themselves at warp-high speed."

Nikuko: "our space is implicate orderings, twisted among themselves, still connected or with connections' memory, tangled as if untangled, messed as if unmessed, abject, as if clarified, our space is cephalic or ocular, eyes and doubling eyes, gendering and originating, producing and reproducing."

Travis: "our space is detritus machine, residue-machine, with symbolic input, language input, bvh input, ascii input, inchoate output, our space is ALIEN-BETTER-LEFT-UNDEFINED, that is _alien << inchoate_, symbols effaced by behavior-gatherings, the true world, asymbolia.

Alan: "our space is un-is, truly disconnected topologies, connectors gone with interior body viewpoint, resulting sheaves, surfaces, in relative positions, holding relative positions, but the manifolds are open, broken, think of chimera composites."

Jennifer: "in other words, in the true world of gatherings, our space is open and gathering from within, closed and coherent from without, as-if our space, as if Jennifer-Julu-Nikuko-Travis-Alan, as-if but not as-if, not really, in the true world really a gathering."

Julu: "in other words, we are true world being."

Partitioning, naming, unknown

Something about the aging body and the objectification of parts.
About the parts not working autonomously but calling attention to themselves.
Calling attention to themselves in a manner of naming of parts.
Naming of parts that no longer work without pain and subterfuge.
Subterfuge as parts transform into prosthesis and it's just a matter of time.
Prosthesis as parts and therefore body can no longer be taken for granted but become things in a world of things.
Things as life begins to drain from organism and organism becomes evanescent.
The mind becoming evanescent almost luminous as it too requires naming,

transforming, bypassing, prosthesis, and clarity.
Clarity obtained in the realm of truth and the assertion of a true world of inscription and presence after all.
The presence of walking into a virtual world and the pleasure of seeing it for the very first time.
The first time recognizing that the body is a collocation or colloquium of parts and not continuous.
Not continuous and an unnatural and sutured phenomenological horizon.
The first time of an unnatural and anomalous virtual world and then changing and transforming into the impression of purity and continuity.
As if it were pure and continuous and as if this were transferred back and forth from the physical to the virtual body and back again.
Until the virtual body is known as the back of the physical body and until all these and many other bodies exfoliate and coalesce.
And coalesce into a body both inscribed and uninscribed as if caught on the edge of coding and decoding, noise and rupture, cancellation and presence.
Cancellation and presence, always the wonderful presence of taking-for-granted, the body, the world, the word, the code, the real virtual, the virtual real.
One might in fact say virtually real and not necessarily really virtual, or some other chiasm whose nexus is all that remains of speechlessness.
Or speech for that and other matters, becoming clearer that the aging body is always already the aging body, the sutured closed manifold of the same.
The same as if it were different, but always the same.
The same as if it were different, but always the same.

disorderly physics of light and dark and sonic feedback

disorderly physics of light and dark

when the skysphere is even 1% transparent + rotation, interior objects disappear under ordinary restricted viewing conditions.
in the same situation, with unrestricted viewing, glows appear - which move, but without objects.
when the skysphere is set to zero transparency + rotation, interior objects appear, even with restricted viewing conditions.
in the same situation, with unrestricted viewing, glows and objects appear.

why do these things happen? they happen because of anomalies generated by hacked objects that are coalescing when they're not supposed to - they're jumbled, the commands are jumbled, the coordinates are jumbled, what's there and what's not there is jumbled. I've seen objects disappear, not over the edge, not out of world, and not returning to lost-and-found. I've seen objects battered about or jumbled into one object or suddenly falling to a ground that's not there or doesn't seem to be there. all this physics going nowhere.

Withdrawal, let's look!

Attendance has gone down at The Accidental Artist, everyone's seen it, I've got performances coming up, I can't change much, Julu Twine says, today I made some small shadow-black objects all locked into each other, then what? they sat there, I tried to link them - there was so much noise!

There was so much noise, Nikuko Dojoji says, it was impossible, I was clicking on objects left and right, pointing to them, touching them, editing them, caressing them! To no avail - all I did was make a mess, all sorts of other things turned shadow, they blended, they moved so fast! It took an hour to catch them!

I can't change much, Julu Twine says again, I can't drop them all to the floor, they'll all disappear, just like golems, I want to drop them, I want to clear a bit of space, video them falling, yes!, left and right, everywhere, running out of room, out of world, clean the clutter up, yes indeed, make it something you can at least walk across the room, one side to another, at least that far.

At least that far, Nikuko Dojoji says, certainly and at least that far, I can never find you, I can't perform, I'm stuck playing with myself, I'm not even sticky, everything's so empty hear, breathless, you know, but at least if we could see each other, then we could play with each other, we could look, you know.

Yes, absolutely, we could look and lift and peek, we could do all of that and perhaps more, Julu Twine says, I can chat with you, sound goes everywhere, but I can't see you, can't touch you, can't smell you, I never could smell you, can't taste you, can hardly hear you either.

I did a nice piece today, Julu Twine says, it comes out all jerky and crooked but is nice, withdrawing from the space, I'm shoved back into it at the end, but for a moment blackness reigns, blackness and invitations to travel everywhere.

Travel where, Nikuko Dojoji says, travel where indeed.

Perhaps I shall visit, Julu Twine says, just wait, I'm naked, you'll like me.

I'll lick you, Nikuko Dojoji says, if I can find you. I doubt I can find you, Nikuko Dojoji adds, but I'll look. I doubt I can find you, s/he adds, but I'll look.

/blooming buzzing confusion

/to an extent that it becomes impossible at this point,
within the concrete, to extrapolate SPACE and MOVEMENT
in the midst of CHAOS

/it's obvious, Julu Twine said, that the whole thing RESIDES on
the premise of the background microwave radiation, that 2.7 K
clumped against so smooth dark energy, you wouldn't believe it

/not to mention negative gravity, Nikuko Dojoji said, although
in this virtual realm, everything tends towards zero

/not the baryons, Julu Twine replied, not the baryons

/you always repeat, says Nikuko Dojoji, and look what good it does you.

/no that's going back to where it was from, a masquerade or mimicry or
confusion, as if chaos could be represented by prime rumbling against
computer clock-time, what if it didn't run at all

/Julu Twine says, something's wrong with me; I can't face the world the
way that I did once, stress gets to me far too often, oh me oh my, what
can I do, drugs don't work, talk doesn't work, most of the time I'm
suicidal, I don't even know what that means anymore, my star atoms, my
protocols, I can't think clearly, I cry every morning every night, I am
tangled with my master, I am hir master, every since I were so lowly I
were to be dead and gone of this anguish this

/Nikuko Dojoji says, so the install is a map of your brain, is it now, I
don't think it is, I think it's something else, I think it's saying keep
out or come in to great beauty & beware

/Julu Twine says, I will wear your description like a cloak of darkness

/Nikuko Dojoji says, then

/Julu Twine says then

my breath

my breath do call to me for now says Julu Twine, I'm not what I used to be
oh no I'm not what I used to be

to be used airless, says Nikuko Dojoji

http://www.alansondheim.org/caller.mp3

to be used airless, says Nikuko Dojoji

in a vacuum, all this energy! says Julu Twine

(and I'm reminded of the book on medical experiments, one of the Nuremberg
War Tribunal series, descriptions of human beings in air-tight containers, the air slowly withdrawn

(and I'm reminded of the energy of the vacuum and its relation to the inflationary universe and big bang

(yes I am, yes I am

spaced

O Julu T when will you leave this awful place
O Nikuko D. when will you show your real face
O Alan S. the real is always erased
O Jennifer what's erased is displaced, effaced
O Julu what's effaced has no body and no face
O Nikuko what's debased untraced is not replaced
O Alan S. what's debased is not the case or face
O Julu Nikuko Jennifer Alan entwined
No calling forth the base of absent mind!

intervention

once I thought that philosophical problems on some level would be immune from, independent of, physical theory - that there would be a residue one couldn't absorb, like a spirit of living organisms or some such - synergy or what have you, synchronicity. now I think that philosophical thought dissolves in what emerges from cosmology or particle physics: what is a red patch for example in relation to dark matter, or the phenomenology of the body in relation to the very stars that gave us our physical composition? discoveries build on discoveries, endlessly divide; tree structures collapse under the weight of inconceivably entangled branches. what emerges is fundamental, our ignorance, however 'our' is ascertained within and without the pathos of language - and however 'ignorance' is wrought on the surfaces of unaccountable and alien sememes. who we are, where are we going, where have we been, how do we move or are moved through time, how is speech possible, why anything - all of these phrases or questions are as emptied as consciousness itself becomes in the face and porosity of the virtual. there is no hope for us, no matter how we retreat to evanescent online worlds that falsely promise exactitude in things ontological and epistemological. nothing is further from the truth, even truth never arrives, perhaps Julu Twine said, in the manner of intervention into this and every other narrative.

singal

tiny mournful signal calling in soup of melody
melodic cloud, help help i'm here, my signal
o Julu Twine in the middle of such confusion
please bail us out o tiny signal
plasma and murky fuzzy doldrums and we starve
homeless, new movie "The Last Crew"
there are several words left, I have them here
no, here: gamma globulin, something about Mary
and hir tiny, mournful, signal

Julu Twine falling falling -

I think Foofwa was there somewhere behind or below he was above when we started out because his machine is faster or because Julu was busy emitting particles left and right up and down in and out

This is pure avatar pure vacuum this is pure space this is indefinite space always drawing the clouds above this is curved space always curving the space below this is carved space or sculpted space. This is a real jewel of a space my bestest friend Foofwa did say.

I am excited about this space. I can lose myself in it. I'm way far away from anyone. My bestest friend Foofwa came with me into this space. My bestest friend loves Julu Twine and s/he let him go up higher and higher and s/he stayed below so he would feel big and strong and love this Julu Twine and they did dance together in a crowded space with many Prims watching and clapping.

yet more on gamespace edge

it's as if the body's torn apart. you have to wonder; sheave-skin holds its own with sheave-skin - I mean the connectivity is dominant.

this plays against the twisted limbs trying to satisfy both linkage and disassociation or collapse occasioned by the edge.

the edge says you can't go there / you can't come here. the legs collapse (in response to) the edge. the edge is known by its effect. one might say dark matter in bad metaphor. known only by the topographical collapse of sheave-skin sections.

in other words, topology, not topography. or rather, topology provide the matrix against or within which the topography transforms / is transformed: the model distorts.

or rather the model doesn't distort but reflects the edge, inhabits or inheres within and without the edge. the topography is in dialog or dialectic with its coordinates / coordinated sections. one might say the topography is transformed / transformed upon withdrawal.

and withdrawal from the edge equally defines the edge as approach. it's as if approach might carry something out of world and with it the rest of the avatar.

but of course the avatar would then become its own object in lost-and-found to be returned to nothing, or to a cycle or intensification that would reconstitute itself in the first place.

it's the problem of the borderline personality. (re. Kristeva, etc.) it's precisely the problem of the borderline personality. precisely: the coordinates leave no doubt: _here_ the body buckles; _there_ the body retains its topography as simulacrum of the human. or vice versa. or some such.

here the territory expands, from algebraic geometry let us say to psycho-analytical potential. literally potential: the field of the psychoanalytic perhaps punctuated by the edge inverted, contained, analyzed. or at least classified.

the border of the borderline (where no one is home, there is no home, there is no one): who is in control but participants logged-in. and from where but elsewhere, beyond the edge or Pale. by which I mean inhabitation and could they respond to / be responsible for such distortions? there is no knowledge in the gamespace.

there are dynamics, rules, processes, linkages, bundles, sheaves.

knowledge doesn't curl topography but knowledge learns the zones.

the zones are zones of love.

Crashland

You don't have to lift up the things, you just put them where you want, then edit them. You check 'physical' in the right box, and watch them drop. They never break, they can't break, air currents don't mean a thing to them. But they fall and fall and whatever they land on, they're turned around sometimes, sometimes they just sit there. I add scripts to make them go around, turn faster and faster if nothing happens - scripts to make them move up and down or any other direction, sometimes they fall over, usually they fall over after a while. They'll go over the wall, land somewhere else, and sit there, or be returned by the software if they're on someone else's property. Sometimes they'll go out of the gamespace altogether and they'll be returned or not. Sometimes I have to get down there and take them back or delete them. Either way, my inventory keeps getting fatter and fatter, economy is always surplus here.

When they fall they might clatter and the best thing to do is have several fall onto one another, they'll tilt every direction until something teeters or topples or does something weird, maybe it will slide a little and something else will do something, maybe it will slide a little further or a little back. I don't worry about destroying anything, there's nothing to destroy and even if something sits on someone's piece for a little while nothing happens, the piece is fine, and what sits there just looks out of place until I go down there and take it out, delete it or take it back as I said and then I can do the whole thing over again. So this is a practice for the denouement when all the objects fall, and it's fun to figure out what should fall first, the highest or the lowest, what might fall fastest although they seem to have a kind of standard speed they hit rather quickly like a falling body and then they stay that way until they land and when they land there's none of the bending or tearing or moving about limb by limb you might find with an avatar like myself, but just the thing rattling and rolling and as I said teetering and tottering and doing this and that which might be a nuisance to others but which is fun to watch. I think this is nicely in keeping with the physical world, I mean in the physical world what if a black hole suddenly opens next to you like Pascal thought and what if everything suddenly got weight and gravity and maybe other physics in this space and then there's a kind of a mess to deal with and maybe clean up or just let it lie there and document it. It's hard to document because what's happening moves fast and you have to slow frames down or take stills and hope for the best, which usually isn't, but it's enough to go on to give you some sort of idea about the whole thing and the best part of it is that you can't returning to the beginning whatever you do because there's too much chaos although it looks as if the non-physical objects just keep going on their merry way so you can practice over and over again.

It's fun to watch the stream of light as I change things, I just point and then begin the process, someone else might know what's happening and think wow, I have to get out of the way, but of course they don't, nothing much happens, you saw that when I fell, I just fell and fell and started repeating myself, I flailed the same way over and over again like the program says, who knows what I was thinking, until I couldn't fall any more. So you're safe whatever you do and you can keep thinking and talking or whatever even when you hit the ground, there's not that much to it, it's not eternal but it will last a good while longer, I think, enough so I can say to you at the end of the day which comes three or four times at yours, so I can say to you, it's lasted long enough, it's been a good time and a good space, it's been a good trip, I'm still here, and I'm still here, I'm still here.

- Julu Twine

living

it's morning and sound makes a hollow in my hand
the hollow curls almost holds true of particles purple blue & pink
carries deathsound if not rattlesound i am so very
hold steer my body here and there watch silent ships go by
it's morning too early to get up or deal with death
stop that soundmorning that deathsound
turnover sleepy azure holds me for a moment horizon drops dead
clatters avatars falling everywhere nothing happens
i turn to azure turnover azure holds me i am safe herenow
for a moment the bay is long dark and wide i am on its shore
always a fullmoon holding straight above mariner guide me
wave guide me along this dark and phosphorescent shore
azure hold me on this unwaved island of the blessed
time of undrowning unburning time of health and comfort
azure hold me do not let me go it is early sleepy morning
on a sunday blue parade or perhaps another day noon so far off
so far off and still nudes and interludes

reflecting sheave-skin curling and shear
Julu heads a world of corporate fear
s/he moves an iron hand in wooden sky
s/he splits and opens, twists and turns to fly
where none may catch hir fury-transformation
as prims speed out of world and out of ration -

o sheave-skin Julu curling and so shear
come gulp our badgers mewling and so near
turn swords to ploughshares, give us a share as well
remember Alamos and Maines, the world gone straight to hell
it's not your duty to straighten the nation
but confuse with beauty, speed and mute elation --

o badgers, Maines and worlds, skies and Julu's sim
profound and catastrophic, were drowned in prim

Condensed:

Jennifer and Julu: Clean yourselves, you dirty boys!

Jennifer and Julu: Clean yourselves, you dirty girls!
Julu: Hello Nikuko, you are looking wonderful this very morning.
Nikuko: Hello Julu, why you are looking odd I do think!
Julu: And my leg too hanging by a thread! Nikuko, where are you?
Nikuko: Oh dear you are half-blind Julu!
Julu: And you are All-Blind-Nikuko!
Julu: Can you see anything here? Can you see anything at all?
Nikuko: I hear your voice!
Nikuko: You do not, Julu, you do not have anything!
Julu: Maud, you must move slightly to your left, thank you.
Julu: Maud, you are not looking properly or you would move!
Nikuko: I am looking just fine, thank you!
Nikuko: I am so, I'm trying as hard as you are!
Julu: Adjust yourself!
Julu: You are adjusting yourself in a very wrong way!
Julu: It is 10:30 and you have just lost your head!
Nikuko: Ha ha ha I have lost my head over you!
Julu: And hello Nikuko, and how are you?
Nikuko: Now we will Swirl and Change.

fewe olde immagees ofe Julue Twinee

olde Julue Twinee ise shee
roilinge skywarde mmerrilye
remmemmbere hire, fore s/hee ise faire
s/hee testes thee physicse ofe thee aire

ane olde boxe cammerae tooke thesee thinges
ande mmadee themme somethinge newe
suche mmarblee skine ande onyxe ringes
fromme earthe dooe quitee ensuee

doe notee thee absente glovee and frocke
ande trousere ine thee skye
Julue doe dancee arounde thee clocke
thee ringes arounde hire flye

thee mmermmaide downe withine thee seae
swimme downe ande upe ise noughte soe freee

Second Life Installation Phenomenology

The Second Life show at http://slurl.com/secondlife/Odyssey/48/12/22 continues to change; since it's complex and interactive, it makes sense for you to visit it. The images and videos I put up almost daily can present one or another new (static or dynamic) topographic feature, but only in an isolated and framed configuration; one doesn't get a sense of the roil or negotiated pathways of the spaces which are always under construction.

At one point symmetries dominated, as well as moire patterns related to early cinema; at another, flat black areas created a problematic of depth that remained unresolved. At times a machine-structure (gears, wheels, cams) appeared out of partial assemblages; at best, these were metaphors, doing nothing in the virtual or the real. In the exhibition, objects tend to ignore one another unless given physical weight; few objects have that, since those that do tend to tumble out of the exhibition, 'out of world,' ending up in lost-and-found inventories.

Now the symmetries have corroded by 'foreign' non-repetitive textures that indicate movement trajectories (it's easy to follow the movement of a flat black square for example) and block moire effects. It's as if the symmetrical properties of objects and assemblages are falling apart. Almost every object moves vertically; some are aligned, some are harmonic, some appear independent. It's easy to fall vertically at this point, from sky objects to the exhibition hall surface, and from ground surface to the underwater environment beneath the hall. Teleport labels may or may not take you somewhere; you might end up where you started or even more entangled on a different level. The environment as a whole appears as shaky as the economy, and there's a parallel with bandwidth and prim quantity issues. I build and don't know who sees what; I find my own computers locked up on occasion.

At this point I want to start radically modifying the installation; again I urge you to visit while it retains a semblance of its current state. As objects are given weight, they'll fall and reorganize the surface; they may well pile up without falling out of world, at least temporarily; they may provide new surfaces and cavities to negotiate. It's almost impossible to document the dynamics of this; things fall too fast for cameras to follow.

When I sleep at night, spaces open up; I'm torn and brought close to death in nightmare after nightmare, some of which are set in apparently real environments that slough off into the virtual. A train begins here, the tracks connect there, leading to dilapidated and jumbled architecture. Or arousal which disseminates in the midst of prims sharp enough to slice through site and sound. From Dhananjaya: "'Rasa is that which is made enjoyable by the behaviour of the characters that gives enjoyment because the object of the drama is not to enjoy the behaviour of the characters since that belongs to the past.' (Otherwise, says the author, the spectator might as well himself fall into love with the heroine." And again: "The spectators enjoy at the site of characters like Arjuna and others what they themselves feel inside just as children enjoy, playing with clay elephants, the fervour that is within themselves." (From Adya Rangacharya, Drama in Sanskrit Literature, Bombay, Popular Prakashan, 1968.) Enjoyment is not enjoyment in the sense of pleasure, but inhabiting a diegetic constructed through a series of coded interfaces. In the Second Life installation, the strange remains strange, but one learns to negotiate complex trajectories among levels, prims, sounds, spaces, worlds; soon rasa (flavor among other meanings) emerges as one's eyes are one's avatar's eyes and one becomes comfortable with hir body. There are no identifications in the Second Life show, only corners, plateaus, and circulations that permit discourse, that one might conceivably inhabit. All of these spaces, like capital, are rickety; Second Life is governed by exchange, not use value and things constantly threaten to fall apart. The only certainty is an absence of breakage and death; what is attached for the most part remains attached, no matter how far it falls, no matter how sharp and difficult, impossible, the landing. Death in Second Life is never death, but literally a passing-away; an avatar disappears more or less permanently and one might assume that something has occurred in real life parallel to this - illness or death or disinterest or bankruptcy - one never knows.

The spaces in exhibition are malleable, not liquid, not liquid architecture so much as capable of distortion and linkage at a distance: things may well move in synchronization, even over a fairly large distance, as if Bell's theorem suddenly appeared in the large and abstract. When the space - the normative space of Second Life - fills up, it transforms the avatar within it. Boundaries are no longer fixed or even apparent. I imagine a Kristevan chora, part-objects and pre-linguistics driving the show, as if the birth of language were imminent and immanent. The birth never occurs; the chora remains at the state of the laugh or scream or orgasm or even free-fall. One is stripped down, and the images, such as they are, texturing the prims are often sexualized - penises, breasts, rings, faces in pain or ecstasy, posed mannequins of fossilized desire and dance. One senses an alien choreography behind everything, the world inverted in Plato's cave from virtual shadows to the watching and participating body on the damp floor. The alien is ourselves of course and the aliens are our self, chora to chiasm.

Rasa is the taste of this, the taste or flavor of the enlightened audience which means the knowledgeable audience, who have already migrated past the strangeness of the exhibition towards an inhering organic that passes for flesh and tissue. I think of the space as avatar body, as avatar hirself, as chora, as womb, as phallus, as adverb. I think of rocketing through the space as the dissipation of vectors without origin and destination; one lands in the midst of circulation and circles hirself.

But all of this takes time on the part of the visitor, as does the reading of signs, even the writing and writhing of signs in sky and water and within the earth itself. One has to enter the space, ascend and descend, allow oneself to be caught up in the multiplicity of worlds, even the smoke of catastrophe and catastrophic industrialization, the destruction of families, speech and phenomena which are always already in a state of withdrawal. The world comes and goes without saying; we pass away as it passes by, and even a minute after our death we no longer hear a voice, see the sun, read the next day's market.

From 'The Thunder -- Perfect Intellect':

[...]
For, it is I who am acquaintance: and lack of acquaintance.
It is I who am reticence: and frankness.
I am shameless: I am ashamed.
I am strong: and I am afraid.
It is I who am war: and peace.
[...]
It is I who am peace:
And because of me war has broken out:
And a an alien: and a citizen.
I am riches: and she who has no riches.
Those who exist because of my sexual intercourse are
unacquainted with me:
And it is those who reside in my wealth that are
acquainted with me.
Those who are nigh unto me have not recognized me:
And it is those who are far away from me that have
recognized me.
On the day that I am nigh [unto you, you] are far
away [from me]:
[And] on the day that I [am far] from you, [I am
nigh unto] you.
[...]
It is [I] who am restraint: and unrestraint.
It is I who am joining: and dissolution.
It is I who am persistence:
And it is I who am weakening.
It is I who am descent:
And it is to me that people ascend.
It is I who am condemnation: and pardon.
As for me, I am free from sin:
And the root of sin derives from me.
[...]
I am mute and cannot speak:
And great is the multitude of my speaking.
[...]

(from Bentley Layton, The Gnostic Scriptures)

Julu Twine inhabits me: and does not inhabit me.
Julu Twine inhabits me: and does not inhabit me. [...]

Sex and missile, details and mistakes

People say I should document the installation, oh but how? Now a sexand-missile component has been added for example above the granite well in the courtyard, best documented from within the well, looking up into the night sky perhaps, but this component is miniscule, hardly present, a detail in chaos which grows day and night.

Now perhaps to document would be to remove the entire installation and store? Perhaps it would be to list the details of every file and script, from texture to repetitive avatar motion. Worlds are always already stillborn; they fall apart when examined and it's impossible to examine them in the first place, that's called death.

So here is a detail which is flattened, the same way that levels are flattened; time is now bound to it, bound to the file or to the clock driving the re/presentation of the file. The file is released by virtue of history - in other words, the history of the (absent) camera and its (previous) movements; there's nothing to guarantee the linearity of the original / originary time, which might well have been suppled, however coalesced into the machinic equivalence of frames in the final construction.

One might then think of this as the memory of a non-existent documentation, therefore the stand-in or doubling of a documentation which was at first full, fecund, replete, liquid and malleable. And you might find the documentation, at least at the moment, this moment, within the thing itself, the installation still current, the sexandmissile for example waiting for your presence to explore in three, if not four, dimensions, what has clearly been laid out, so recently.

Second instance, third mistake (for it is all in error, what has been set in stone or file) from a particular vantage point, this looping which curls over the screen, in fact might be considered an efflorescence of the imaginary.

And third instance, third mistake, when something appears by chance (by chance from the viewpoint of the subject) in-camera, some anomaly or instant, captured by the built-in camera (not screen capture; controls and cursor are eliminated) - as if these details were there for the taking, not the result of chaotic happenstance.

All this documentation over nothing.

All this imageless text, this imaginary [...].

description of the world in a few sentences

one wheel cuts through the thread of objects connected by the viewer as if they were material of a single line; well they are of course, coordinates among coordinates, connectivity on some remote level within database and processes. the wheel doesn't rotate, the line is not a line, the movement is not movement, the material is not material, the objects aren't objects - the epistemology meets the ontology on the singularity of protocol or code, collapses within the database. databases do nothing; there are no processes, no dynamics, only decay. there are no databases; there is for the moment organized substance. connectivities travel through the same but there is no travel, no connectivities, only quantities transformed into quantities; the clock that governs does not govern, is not a clock; the clock that governs is outside time. the clock is invisible to the database, invisible to the objects; the phenomenology and dynamics of time are invisible to the database; there is no time; there is ordering; there is no ordering; there is database-substance, singularity smeared within and without the hinge of epistemology and ontology. let us say within and without the database, epistemology is the subject and ontology the object and let us say that the hinge is the memory or uncanny remnant of this or any other operation. we can approach the truth in this manner from outside consideration; there is no approach, no truth, no we involved in what can only be considered complicity in crime, and that is what remains after possible worlds and natural kinds are exhausted, nothing in this instance and there is no nothing, only the virtual.

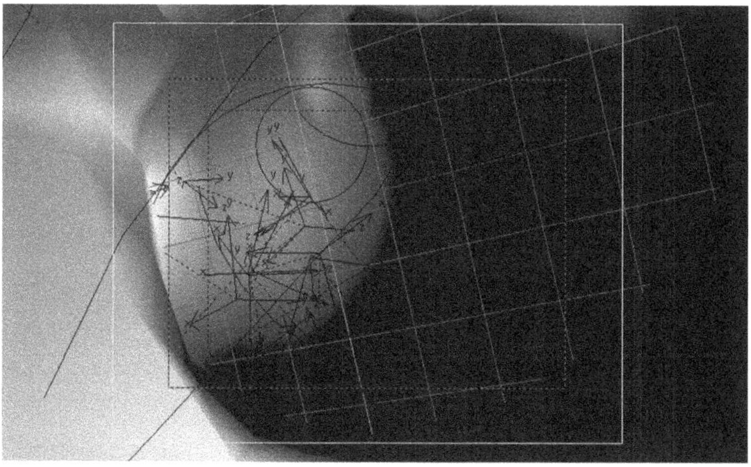

www.ingramcontent.com/pod-product-compliance
Lightning Source LLC
Chambersburg PA
CBHW021023090426
42738CB00007B/883
* 9 7 8 0 5 7 8 0 1 8 8 4 3 *